D&S
VOL. 53

Covers all
of the U.S
torpedo b...

...er
...r II

TBF/TBM
Avenger

in detail & scale

Bert Kinzey

squadron/signal publications

This book is a product of Detail & Scale, Inc., which has sole responsibility for its content and layout, except that all contributors are responsible for the security clearance and copyright release of all materials submitted. Published by Squadron/Signal Publications, 1115 Crowley Drive, Carrollton, Texas 75011.

CONTRIBUTORS AND SOURCES:

Lloyd Jones	Paul Gold	National Museum of Naval Aviation, Pensacola, Florida
Jim Roeder	John Bruning, Sr.	U. S. Marine Corps Museum of Aviation, Quantico, Virginia
Jeff Ethell	The Collings Foundation	USS Yorktown, CV-10, Museum, Patriots Point, South Carolina
Larry Webster	Grumman Aerospace Corporation	Museum of Aviation, Warner Robins, Georgia
Charles Gallo	Eastern Aircraft Corporation	Planes of Fame Museum, Chino, California
Joe Szokoli	National Archives	War Eagles Museum, Santa Teresa, New Mexico
Stan Parker	U. S. Navy	Yanks Museum, Chino, California

Many photographs in this publication are credited to their contributors. Photographs with no credit indicated were taken by the author.

Detail & Scale, Inc. and the author extend a very special word of thanks to Bob Collings of the Collings Foundation for his cooperation and timely assistance during the preparation of this publication.

Special thanks are also due to Hill Goodspeed of the National Museum of Naval Aviation, Mike Starn of the Marine Corps Museum of Aviation, and to Bill Paul of the Museum of Aviation at Warner Robins.

DEDICATION:
TO MY FRIEND, DON HORTON

Don Horton was a radio-operator/gunner in TBD-1 Devastators from before World War II through the Battle of Midway. He flew with ENS I. H. McPherson in TBD-1, BuNo. 0368, during the Battle of Midway. With T-5 painted on its side, this Devastator was one of the few that survived that decisive battle. Don later flew as a turret gunner in TBF-1 Avengers while assigned to the reformed VT-6. Don was flying from the USS HORNET, CV-8, when it was sunk at the Battle of the Santa Cruz Islands. He later serviced Avengers as an aircraft mechanic aboard the USS SANGAMON, CVE-26. After the war, Don Horton was a technical representative for the United States Army Missile Command. In 1971 and 1972, the author was a captain in the Army and was the Missile Systems Officer for the 3rd Battalion (HAWK) 68th Air Defense Artillery. During most of that time, Don was assigned to the author's section as the MICOM representative, and he shared his remarkable and unforgetable wartime experiences with a grateful and eager listener.

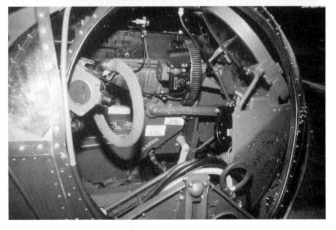

Above (front cover photo): The pilot of a TBF-1C is about to start his engine in preparation for a mission during the Marshalls/Gilberts Campaign. The photo was taken aboard the USS MONTEREY, CVL-26, on December 10, 1943. *(National Archives)*

Above right (rear cover, top photo): The pilot's cockpit in the Collings Foundation's restored TBM-3E looks very much like it did when the aircraft rolled off the production line.

Right (rear cover, bottom photo): The Collings Foundation accurately restored the colors and details of the turret on their Avenger to original specifications.

INTRODUCTION

A TBM-3E is ready to launch from the port catapult of the USS PHILIPPINE SEA, CV-47. (John M. Moore via NMNA)

By the end of 1987, over two dozen books had been released in the Detail & Scale Series. But the B-17 Flying Fortress and the B-29 Superfortress were the only two aircraft from World War II that had been included. This was due largely to the difficulty in finding the detailed photographs of all variants of a World War II aircraft that would be necessary to provide comprehensive coverage in one of our publications.

The books on the B-17 and B-29 had been done by Al Lloyd, an employee of Boeing who had access to the extensive historical archives at that company. Most other aircraft manufacturers from the World War II time period no longer existed or had been absorbed by other companies. Most of those who were still in business did not have much in the way of historical photos, and what photos did exist were of a general nature rather than being the necessary detailed photographs.

One exception was Grumman Aerospace at Bethpage, Long Island. For many years, Grumman had maintained an excellent history center under the capable direction of "Schoney" Schonenberg and Lois Lovisolo. Detail & Scale had already worked with this fine facility during the research and preparation for books on the Grumman's F9F Panther, F9F Cougar, and F11F Tiger.

In late 1987, the author traveled to New York to look through the center's files on the F4F Wildcat, F6F Hellcat, and TBF/M Avenger in hopes of adding these World War II aircraft to the Detail & Scale Series. Excellent resources, including sufficient detailed photographs, were obtained on the Wildcat and Hellcat, but the files for the Avenger were minimal. There were almost no detailed photographs, and what general photos were available had been published numerous times before. As a result, Detail & Scale produced publications on the Wildcat and Hellcat in 1988, but it looked as though the Avenger would not

be included in the series.

In 1995, quite by accident, the author discovered the delivery photographs of the Avenger as supplied to the Navy by both Grumman and Eastern. These delivery files had scores of excellent photographs showing every imaginable detail on the aircraft. All major wartime variants were included, and this made a Detail & Scale book on the Avenger possible.

In addition to the discovery of the manufacturers' photographs, the excellent restoration of several Avengers has also played a significant role in the development of this book. No less than eight Avengers at seven different museums were photographed for this publication. Care was used to insure that the photos taken of these aircraft accurately depicted what operational aircraft looked like during World War II. When minor discrepancies did exist, they have been pointed out in the captions.

Combining the manufacturers' photographs with those taken by several photographers specifically for this Detail & Scale book has resulted in the most detailed look at the Avenger ever published. Additionally, aviation researcher Lloyd Jones has developed new scale drawings specifically for this book. Major differences between variants are pointed out on these drawings.

With excellent 1/72nd and 1/48th scale models of the Avenger having been released by Hasegawa and Accurate Miniatures, this publication will be very valuable to scale modelers as well as to aviation enthusiasts. These kits, along with all others of the Avenger, are covered in the Modelers Section at the end of the book.

Many people and organizations made significant contributions and provided valuable assistance during the preparation of this book. Their names are listed on page 2, and Detail & Scale, Inc. and the author express a sincere word of thanks to them all.

3

HISTORICAL SUMMARY

The pilot of a TBF-1 follows the hand signals of a deck crewman as he taxis into position for launch. Other Avengers, with their wings still folded, wait for their turns further aft on the flight deck. **(National Archives)**

It was nicknamed "Turkey," and its combat debut was a disaster. It was a torpedo bomber, but it carried bombs much more often than torpedoes. It was flown by George Bush, a future President of the United States, and by countless brave young men whose names will never be known publicly. Flying from small escort carriers in the Atlantic, it dropped depth charges on German U-boats. In the Pacific, it torpedoed and sunk the largest Japanese battleships, bombed enemy positions on islands and atolls, and fired rockets in support of allied troops on the ground. In living up to its name, the Avenger proved to be one of the most successful and versatile aircraft of the Second World War.

In the post-war years, the Avenger's large airframe was modified for special roles ranging from early-warning radar platforms to submarine killers, and from carrier onboard delivery aircraft to target tugs. It became one of the world's first electronic jamming platforms, and when their military service was finished, civilian Avengers fought forest fires in the United States and Canada.

By the late 1930s, the United States Navy had moved out of the biplane era for all of its carrier-based aircraft. The F4F Wildcat fighter, SBD Dauntless dive bomber, and TBD Devastator torpedo bomber were all metal-skinned monoplanes. All had entered service during the latter half of the decade, but with the possibility of a naval war against Japan becoming more likely with each passing month, the Navy was already ordering replacements for all three of these aircraft. Although Hellcat and Corsair fighters, as well as Helldiver dive bombers, joined the war effort as first line aircraft, improved versions of both the Wildcat and Dauntless continued to serve until the Japanese surrendered in September 1945. But with the TBD Devastator, it was a different story.

The Devastator had joined the fleet in 1937, and deliveries of 129 TBD-1s had been completed by 1939. No subsequent orders for additional TBD-1s or any improved versions were ever placed. Don Horton, who joined VT-6 as a radio operator/gunner/mechanic in the pre-war years, and who later survived the Battle of Midway in the rear seat of a Devastator, recalled that it was a "nice airplane to fly, but it was very slow." Don remem-

bered seeing pilots stand up in the cockpit during flights in order to wipe off the windscreen with a rag. When Don worked for the author in the early 1970's, he fondly remembered the Devastator saying, "In spite of all its limitations, we really loved that airplane, and we had a special relationship with it."

Because of its terrible loss rate at the Battle of Midway, the Devastator has received a lot of unfair criticism. After all, of the six new Avengers that participated in that same battle, five were shot down, and only one limped back to Midway Island where it was written off. In both cases, the extreme loss rate experienced by the torpedo bombers was because they attacked the Japanese fleet without air cover and without coordination with dive bombers. Flying low, slow, and alone in their attacks, they were sitting ducks for Japanese fighters and anti-aircraft guns.

The Devastator had performed satisfactorily in the hit-and-run raids of early 1942 and at the first major carrier battle in the Coral Sea. Their loss rates had been quite acceptable when serving as horizontal bombers as well as torpedo bombers up until the Battle of Midway.

But the big problem with the Devastator, along with its lack of speed, was that it did not have armor protection and self-sealing fuel tanks. Accordingly, it was not truly a combat-ready aircraft. It carried its torpedo externally in a semi-recessed bay under the fuselage, and its bomb load was restricted to small bombs carried under the wings. All of these basic shortcomings caused the Navy to publish new requirements for a replacement in 1939 when the last deliveries of TBD-1s were just reaching operational units.

The new requirements called for a top speed of 300 miles-per-hour and a range of 3,000 miles as a scout. Both conventional bombs and torpedoes were to be carried in an internal weapons bay. The aircraft was to have armor protection for the crew and vital areas, and fuel tanks had to be self-sealing.

Vought proposed the XTBU-1 Sea Wolf, while the Grumman entry was the XTBF-1. On April 8, 1940, two XTBF-1 prototypes were ordered, and a contract was issued for 286 production TBF-1s in December of that year. Both the urgency of the situation and the Navy's faith in the design were reflected in this initial order, because it came eight months before the maiden flight of the first prototype.

The XTBF-1 was lighter and faster than Vought's XTBU-1, and it could fly further. Although quite large for a carrier-based aircraft, it was less than nineteen feet wide when the wings were folded. More importantly, Grumman had the ability to begin deliveries almost as soon as they received approval, while Vought's resources were strained as that company tried to sort out the problems with its F4U Corsair. The Navy needed a torpedo bomber right away, and Grumman had the capability to begin deliveries sooner than Vought. As a result, the XTBF-1 was selected over the Sea Wolf.

The XTBF-1 was the first torpedo bomber that Grumman had ever produced, and it relied heavily on the proven design of the F4F Wildcat fighter. But there were some new innovations as well. The Navy wanted to move away from radio operators doubling as gunners in open cockpits. Enclosed power-operated turrets offered a better alternative when it came to defensive firepower. Curtiss had tried and failed to find an established turret manufacturer to produce a turret for its XSB2C Helldiver, which, like Vought's Corsair, was having a number of developmental problems. A suitable turret was never found for the Helldiver, so Curtiss was forced to retain an antiquated .30-caliber flexible-gun mount in an open rear cockpit as the defensive armament for the SB2C.

But the engineers at Grumman figured they could design a suitable turret for the XTBF-1 themselves. Using electricity to power the unit, rather than hydraulics as had been used on larger designs, Grumman came up with an effective turret for its new torpedo bomber.

The Devastator had a single .30-caliber machine gun in the open rear cockpit as did early production versions of the Dauntless. A "strap-together" twin mount with two .30-caliber guns was retrofitted to TBD-1s and most SBDs just prior to the Battle of Midway, and it would become standard in Dauntlesses during the SBD-3 production run.

By comparison, the new turret for the Avenger had only a single machine gun because of the necessity to keep it small and light enough to fit in the aircraft's fuselage. But it was a .50-caliber weapon, and with the increased energy and penetrating capability of the larger round, one .50-caliber machine gun proved to be more deadly than two .30-caliber weapons in combat. It also meant that the gunner could begin engaging an attacking aircraft at a greater range. Don Horton, who later served as a turret gunner in Avengers, recounted how the turret was far more effective than even the twin guns in the Devastator, but the open cockpit was more fun---until the shooting started!

Grumman did retain a .30-caliber defensive gun in the radio compartment to protect the aircraft from below. The radio operator would man the enclosed position whenever hostile aircraft were in the Avenger's vicinity.

Forward-firing armament was a single .30-caliber machine gun mounted on the right side of the cowling. This would prove to be a major shortcoming, and it was deleted in favor of two .50-caliber guns in the wings beginning with TBF-1C production.

As specified in the Navy requirement, the XTBF-1 had an internal weapons bay that could carry a 2,000-pound torpedo or a combination of bombs. Up front, a Wright R-2600-8 radial engine provided 1,700 horsepower. Although this was a reliable powerplant, operational use would reveal that its power was barely sufficient. During the Avenger's service, Wright increased the horsepower to 1,900 with the R-2600-20, while Grumman and Eastern tried to reduce the weight of the aircraft.

The first XTBF-1 prototype made its initial flight on August 7, 1941, with Grumman's test pilot, Robert L. Hall, at the controls. Flight testing continued until the aircraft was destroyed in a crash on November 28. It was replaced by the second prototype less than three weeks later on December 15. But the urgency to get the aircraft into service was now heightened, because in the interim Japan had attacked Pearl Harbor.

During early flight testing, a lack of directional stability was detected. This was corrected by the addition of a large dorsal fin on the spine of the aircraft. Another problem was a tail-heavy center of gravity. Solving this problem involved moving the engine forward twelve inches.

By the time the second prototype had made a dozen flights, aircraft started rolling off the production line. Deliveries to the Navy began in January 1942, and a detachment of VT-8 was the first unit to receive the new aircraft. In May, after working out a few problems with their new aircraft, this detachment headed west in hopes of catching up with the USS HORNET, CV-8. They arrived in Hawaii on May 29, but the carrier had departed for Midway the day before. The remainder of VT-8 was still aboard, equipped with their TBD-1 Devastators.

With the red and white stripes on their rudders painted out, six of the TBF-1s were flown to Midway Island on the first of June with LT Langdon K. Fieberling in command. Three days later they would become the first Avengers to experience combat.

On June 4, the six TBF-1s flew out to attack the Japanese fleet. Five of the six Avengers were shot down, and only ENS Albert K. "Bert" Earnest, in BuNo. 03805 headed back to Midway Island. With his turret gunner killed and his radio operator wounded, Earnest flew the Avenger with only the trim tabs to control the elevators. His main controls had been shot away, and the hydraulic system was gone. Without hydraulics, the tail wheel hung down from the fuselage and prevented the stinger gun from being used. This left the Avenger defenseless as enemy fighters continued to make runs on 8-T-1. But Earnest managed to get his crippled aircraft back to Midway Island where it was written off. Eighteen men had set out to attack the Japanese in the six Avengers. When it was over, only two of them, Earnest and his radio operator, Harry H. Ferrier, survived.

If nothing else, the Avenger's combat debut at Midway proved how rugged the aircraft was. With more than seventy bullet holes in his aircraft, with his elevator controls shot away, the bomb bay doors hanging open, with no hydraulics and no compass, Earnest was still able to get the big torpedo bomber back to his base. His skills earned him the Navy Cross, and the survival of his aircraft provided valuable information about the Avenger in combat.

Thirteen of VT-2's TBD-1s had gone down with the USS LEXINGTON, CV-2, when the carrier was sunk at the Battle of the Coral Sea. All fifteen of VT-8s Devastators

Underside details are revealed as an Avenger banks away from the camera. **(National Archives)**

As the TBF-1s rolled off the production line, they were rushed to these units which were quickly reformed. New squadrons for the growing carrier fleet were also commissioned and made combat ready. By August 1942, all torpedo squadrons aboard carriers in the Pacific had received their Avengers. As they reformed, the squadrons went where they were needed rather than to the carrier to which they had long been assigned. HORNET's VT-8, which had been wiped out at Midway, was operating from the USS SARATOGA, CV-3. SARA's VT-3 was aboard ENTERPRISE, and the Big "E's" VT-6 was embarked in HORNET.

The first carrier-based attack flown by Avengers was made by VT-3 when two TBF-1s spotted the Japanese carrier RYUJO during a scouting mission. They dropped four 500-pound bombs on the Japanese flattop, but none scored a hit. ENTERPRISE launched a follow-up attack with more Avengers and Dauntlesses. The Avengers launched torpedoes while the SBDs plunged down on the carrier to deliver their bombs. The coordinated effort sent RYUJO to the bottom.

Meanwhile, the Marines were also forming torpedo squadrons, and the first of these was rushed to Guadalcanal. By November 1942, TBF-1s were flying from Henderson Field as part of Guadalcanal's "Cactus Air Force." VMSB-131 (later VMTB-131) was the first unit to fly Avengers from Henderson Field, and their TBF-1s helped sink the Japanese battleship HIEI.

By the end of 1942, 646 Avengers had been produced. But the demands for more and more aircraft would gradually cause a shift in Avenger production to General Motors' Eastern Aircraft Division. The Navy's priority was for first line fighters, and it wanted Grumman's plant to concentrate on the production of the F6F Hellcat. As a result, Eastern geared up to take over responsibility of building the Avenger and the Wildcat. The Navy assigned Eastern the letter "M" as its manufacturer's identification, thus the Eastern-built Avengers were designated TBMs.

In November 1942, Eastern produced its first TBM-1s, and by mid-1943, Avengers were coming off Eastern's production lines at the rate of more than 100 per month. By the end of 1943, Grumman's Avenger production had ceased, leaving the responsibility entirely with Eastern.

To protect convoys in the Atlantic, both the U. S. and British developed small escort carriers. Many of the CVEs

were shot down at Midway. SARATOGA's VT-3 flew from the USS YORKTOWN, CV-5, during the Battle of Midway. Twelve of thirteen TBD-1s were launched, and only one of these returned. VT-6 in ENTERPRISE, CV-6, launched fourteen Devastators against the Japanese at Midway, and only three of these returned to the ship. One of these three was so badly shot up that it was pushed over the side.

Between May 7 and June 4, 1942, the U. S. Navy lost four of its torpedo squadrons and the bulk of its operational TBD-1 Devastators. All that was left in the Pacific were VT-5, which was at Pearl Harbor with seven aircraft, and VT-7 which was aboard the USS WASP, CV-7, with only four TBD-1s. USS RANGER, CV-4, was operating in the Atlantic with eight Devastators.

Not all Avengers operated from carriers. Both Navy and Marine squadrons flew missions from shore bases as shown here. The first such land-based use of the Avenger was from Henderson Field during the battle for Guadalcanal. **(National Archives)**

In spite of its large size, the Avenger operated effectively from small escort carriers in both the Atlantic and Pacific theaters. The CVEs, with their composite squadrons of Wildcats and Avengers, provided the vital convoys with effective protection against German U-boats. Both Wildcats and Avengers can be seen here as they prepare for launch from the USS SANTEE, CVE-29. The aircraft are painted in the Dark Gull Gray over white paint scheme used in the Atlantic. (National Archives)

were simply flight decks that had been built over the modified hulls of merchant ships, although some later classes were built as escort carriers from the keel up. Regardless, these "baby flattops" were much smaller than the fleet carriers or even the light carriers then in service. They were intended to carry a small composite air wing of about twenty-one aircraft consisting of a combination of fighters and bombers. The small Wildcat proved ideal for duty aboard the CVEs but the early use of the SBD Dauntless was less than satisfactory. Although the Dauntless was a relatively small aircraft, it lacked folding wings. This restricted the number of aircraft that could be stored in the limited space of the escort carrier's hangar bay. The Avenger, with its folding wings, easily fit on the elevators of the small carriers, and more of them could be stored on the hangar deck than was the case with the Dauntless.

Fortunately, by the time escort carriers became available in numbers during 1943, there was a sufficient quantity of Avengers to be used in their air groups. Although some of the early Wildcats and Avengers that flew from these escort carriers were built by Grumman, by 1944, Eastern was producing every Wildcat and Avenger that was being assigned to the CVEs.

The first escort carrier to operate with this mixed air group was the USS BOGUE, CVE-9. Composite Air Wing Nine (VC-9) initially had twelve Wildcats and eight TBF-1s, but the mix was changed to nine Wildcats and twelve Avengers. Aboard fleet carriers in the Pacific, fighters were more important, and the percentage of fighters in their air groups continually increased throughout the war. But in the Atlantic, where air superiority was not a major factor, it was soon realized that it was important to have more bombers. The Avenger, with its long range and good payload capability, proved to be very adept in patrolling the ocean around the convoys. When a U-boat was found, it could drop general purpose or depth bombs on the target. Later, rockets and Fido homing torpedoes were added to its anti-submarine arsenal.

BOGUE's first attacks came in May 1943, and the first confirmed sinking of a Nazi U-boat was on May 22 when U-569 was destroyed by depth bombs dropped by one of VC-9's Avengers. VC-9 would go on to be the leading killer of U-boats among the escort carriers with eight confirmed sinkings. A total of thirty German submarines were sunk by the small composite air wings aboard the escort carriers in the Atlantic. Avengers shared two kills with surface ships as well. On June 4, 1944, the hunter-killer team working with the USS GUADALCANAL, CVE-60, forced U-505 to the surface where it was cap-

At left, a TBF-1 is lined up on the catapult aboard the USS SANTEE as it begins another sub-hunting mission. In the photograph at right, deck crewmen scurry around a TBF-1C as it is readied for launch. (Both National Archives)

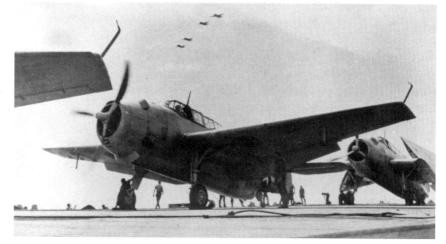

TBF-1s line up for launch from a carrier while others circle overhead waiting for the rest of the flight to join them. (Jones collection)

tured.

But the primary purpose of the escort carriers was not to sink German submarines. Their mission was to protect the ships in the convoys, and providing protection did not necessarily mean the submarines had to be sunk. Simply keeping them away from the slow venerable merchant ships was really protection enough. Throughout the remainder of the war, the ever increasing number of American and British escort carriers did just that. Even when no submarines were attacked, the mere presence of the CVEs and their patrolling aircraft made the U-boat's job far more difficult and thus significantly reduced the number of convoy losses. Aircraft from the CVE's air group also worked with the convoy's destroyer escorts and thereby improved the overall effectiveness of the anti-submarine team.

By the end of 1943, Avengers were serving aboard escort carriers in the Pacific as well as the Atlantic. Every fleet and light carrier had Avengers in their air groups, and an increasing number of Navy and Marine shore-based units were operating the aircraft.

By this time, production had changed over to the TBF-1C and TBM-1C with increased firepower to the front of the aircraft. Operational experience had revealed the obvious inadequacy of the single .30-caliber machine gun in the cowling, so this had been replaced with two .50-caliber weapons in the wings. The instruments and accommodations in the second cockpit had been deleted in favor of more radio and other electronic equipment.

BuNo. 00393 had a Wright R-2600-10 engine installed for evaluation purposes, and it was designated the XTBF-2. However, no production TBF-2s or TBM-2s were built.

The more powerful TBM-3 was the next production variant, and it was equipped with the R-2600-20 engine with 200 more horsepower than the -8 used in the earlier versions. The lighter TBM-3E, with its APS-4 radar, began joining the fleet in 1944.

Three XTBM-4 prototypes were built in 1945. Similar to the TBM-3E, these aircraft had a stronger wing and an improved wing folding mechanism. As the war ended, production of the TBM-4 was cancelled before it began.

One measure of the Avenger's success in the Pacific is its contribution to the sinking of the enemy's major

In its original specifications for a new torpedo bomber, the Navy stipulated that the aircraft would have to be able to serve as a scout bomber. To keep these "eyes in the sky" in the air at any time, several ESSEX class carriers were fitted with catapults in their hangar decks. These catapults ran laterally across the hangar just aft of the forward elevator. During recovery operations, launches were not possible from the flight deck, because returning aircraft had to be spotted forward. However, scouts and their escorting fighters could still be launched from these hangar deck catapults. At left, a TBF-1 is hooked up to the hangar deck catapult aboard the USS YORKTOWN, CV-10, while the photo at right shows the aircraft as it is launched through the hangar deck and out the other side of the ship. (Both National Archives)

This TBM-3 is from VT-6 which operated from the USS HANCOCK, CV-19, during 1945. Nose art, in the form of two dice, can be seen on the forward fuselage.   *(National Archives)*

surface combatants. The Imperial Japanese Navy lost twenty-six aircraft carriers to all causes during the war. Five of these were lost before the Avenger became operational (excepting the six TBF-1s used at Midway Island). Of the remaining nineteen carriers, Avengers contributed to the sinking of twelve. Out of eleven battleships lost by Japan, Avengers were involved in the sinking of six. Nineteen of forty-one crusiers lost by Japan in World War II were sunk completely or in part by Avengers. They also were involved in the sinking of twenty-five destroyers and scores of smaller craft. When this impressive tally is added to the attacks against Japanese bases on Pacific islands and atolls, the countless missions flown in support of Allied forces on the ground, and the many other less

glamorous but important tasks performed by the Avenger, its considerble value to the war effort is easily appreciated.

Other than the United States, the major user of Avengers during World War II was the Royal Navy's Fleet Air Arm. The British originally called the aircraft the Tarpon, but this was changed to Avenger in January 1944. A total of 958 Avengers were delivered to the Fleet Air Arm, and they served in fourteen squadrons of the Royal Navy. British Avengers were modified by Blackburn Aircraft, Ltd. where British gun sights, radios, and oxygen equipment were added. The British also retained the seat in the second cockpit in all of their aircraft, and they added a blistered sighting window to

The Fleet Air Arm of the Royal Navy was the other major operator of Avengers during World War II. Until January 1944, the British called the aircraft the Tarpon, but this was later changed to Avenger as the Royal Navy began to operate more closely with the U. S. Navy. At left, Tarpon Mk Is are shown at a shore base, while at right, British crews check out a new Tarpon. The blistered side window, common to British Avengers, is all but obscured by the head of the man bending over. One squadron of Avengers also operated with the Royal New Zealand Air Force during the war. Several more nations acquired Avengers in the post-war years.

(Both National Archives)

The final paint scheme used on Avengers during World War II was the overall Sea Blue scheme as seen on this TBM-3E. A white APS-4 radar pod can be seen beneath the right wing. The three vertical stripes on the tail indicate that this aircraft was assigned to VT-89 when that squadron operated from the USS ANTIETAM, CV-36, in 1945. **(National Archives)**

each side of the aft fuselage. The only other nation to fly Avengers during the Second World War was New Zealand, which operated one squadron.

Avengers, up through the TBM-3, had an ASB radar with its associated YAGI antennas as standard equipment, but some were modified and had special radars installed. Several experiments with these radars were conducted during the war. Most notable of these was the nighttime use of a single Avenger with two Hellcat fighters. The radar in the Avenger was used to locate Japanese aircraft in the darkness, and the Hellcats would be directed to the intercept. It was in one of these early experiments that Metal of Honor recipient Edward "Butch" O'Hare was accidently shot down and killed. Exact details of the event have never been known, but it appears that O'Hare was mistaken for an enemy and shot down by the turret gunner as he reformed on the Avenger after an intercept.

A few TBF-1s and -1Cs were fitted with the ASD-1 radar and used as TBF-1D night bombers. They often retained their ASB radars and YAGI antennas as well. TBM-3s were likewise converted to TBM-3Ds. Armament was sometimes removed from these aircraft to save weight during night operations. Although there were a couple of instances where two or three of these night bombers were assigned to regular torpedo squadrons aboard SAN JACINTO, CVL-30, and WASP, CV-18, most of them operated from dedicated night carriers. USS INDEPENDENCE, CVL-22, became the first night carrier, while SARATOGA, CV-3, and ENTERPRISE, CV-6, followed.

The Avenger was the last torpedo bomber ordered into production by the United States Navy. In the post-war years, a few remained in service in this role, but more were converted as special purpose aircraft. A summary of these modifications and conversions can be found on pages 31 and 32.

A number of foreign nations obtained Avengers for use in their air arms after World War II. These included Great Britain, which like the United States, modified many of their aircraft for special missions. Canada, France, The Netherlands, and Uruguay all acquired Avengers, and those in the Royal New Zealand Air Force continued in operation. In the mid-1950s, when Japan began rebuilding its military as the Japanese Self-Defense Force, it too obtained twenty Avengers. Thus, the nation the Avenger had helped to defeat later operated TBM-3W and TBM-3S versions in its own military forces.

As Avengers were disposed of by the military, many were converted into aerial tankers to fight forest fires. Both civilian-owned companies and the federal government acquired surplus Avengers for this purpose.

Almost 10,000 Avengers were produced. While only a handful remain today, it is fortunate that some are in museums where they are preserved very much as they were in World War II. Several are in private hands and remain airworthy. These have been restored to varying levels of authenticity, although recently it seems that more care has been taken to make these restorations as accurate as possible and still keep the aircraft flyable. Most existing Avengers are TBM-3 or -3E aircraft. Only two Grumman-built TBF-1s are known to exist. One of these is at the National Air and Space Museum's Silver Hill facility, while the other is at the Yanks Air Museum in Chino, California. Both are awaiting restoration. Hopefully, they will soon be restored to original specifications just as they appeared during the desperate days of 1942 when they were built. That would be a fitting tribute to both the men and the machine that did so much to defeat the Axis during World War II.

On April 19, 1949, this TBM-3E crashed while landing on the USS SIBONEY, CVE 112. The pilot, ENS Daniel M. Morris suffered minor injuries, as did SA Arian D. Willock, who was one of the crew members. The other crewman, ENS John W. Wested was not injured. AFAN John L. Powell, who was standing on the search platform, was killed in the accident. **(Beeler via Webster)**

MOCK-UP

The mock-up for the Avenger was made mostly of plywood. The original design called for a pitot boom to be located on the leading edge of the left wing. This was subsequently changed to the L-shaped probe on the wing tip as used on all Avenger variants.
(Grumman)

The original arrangement for the windows on the aft fuselage can be seen in these two views. Also note the lack of a dorsal fin on the spine of the aircraft. This feature was not added until after the first few flights of the original prototype. The engine section was twelve inches shorter in the original design, but it was lengthened after flight testing of the first prototype indicated that the aircraft was tail heavy.
(Both Grumman)

Although the mock-up had only the left wing, it did fold to illustrate how compact the aircraft would be for storage on a carrier. (Grumman)

XTBF-1

Two XTBF-1 prototypes were built and flight tested extensively by Grumman. These tests indicated that very few changes were necessary, so the first production TBF-1s were almost identical to these aircraft.   (Grumman)

Note the initial production design and position of the windows on the aft fuselage in these two views. The soundness of the design can be illustrated by comparing the photographs on this page with other photos of the final TBM-3Es produced in 1945. There were no major design modifications in the Avenger throughout the entire production of almost 10,000 aircraft. Only relatively minor detail changes to the antenna mast, armament, radar installation, tail hook, cowl flaps, and cowling air scoops were made as subsequent variants were introduced.   (Both Grumman)

Above: The antenna mast on an XTBF-1 is shown here in detail. It was mounted in the forward position and angled back slightly. This design was carried forward on the TBF-1, but it was changed on all subsequent versions. A measuring instrument has been attached to the top of this mast.   (Grumman)

Right: The details of the R-2600-8 engine, as used on the XTBF-1, TBF-1, and TBF-1C, are visible here. The propeller cuffs on the prototypes were natural metal.   (Grumman)

XTBF-1 COCKPIT DETAILS

The instrument panel in the XTBF-1s was very basic. Although the cockpit was quite spacious, all essential items were within easy reach of the pilot. (Grumman)

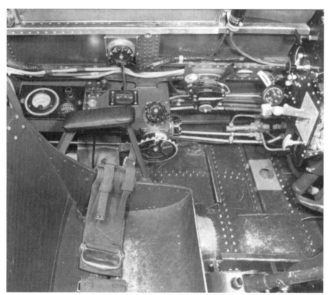

The left side of the pilot's cockpit had the throttle quadrant in the usual position. Landing gear and flap levers can be seen at right. From the very beginning, arm rests were installed on the seat to help reduce fatigue on long flights. (Grumman)

The electrical distribution panel and radio gear occupied most of the cockpit's right side. (Grumman)

The center panel is seen here as is the location where the control column attaches to the airframe. This would usually be covered by a canvas boot. (Grumman)

Both the XTBF-1 and the TBF-1 had a seat in a second cockpit located just behind the pilot's cockpit. Basic instruments were provided, but there were no flight controls. Note that the seat was mounted closer to the left side of the cockpit. (Grumman)

TBF-1 & TBM-1

The first production Avenger was the TBF-1. Early examples had red and white stripes painted on the rudder, but these were painted out before any aircraft reached the combat zones. This aircraft is painted in the Blue-Gray over light gray paint scheme, and small national insignias are used in six positions. Also note the aft fuselage windows. Originally, there were three windows on each side as shown here. The forward window was a small rectangle, and it was located just aft of and slightly below the trailing edge of the wing. It was deleted on later TBF-1s and all subsequent versions. The middle window was circular, as shown here, on early TBF-1s, but on all subsequent aircraft it was oval and located closer to the wing. A larger blistered window was used instead on British aircraft. The aft window remained the same on all variants.
(Grumman)

The first production version of the Avenger was the TBF-1, and these aircraft were essentially the same as the second XTBF-1 prototype. Early examples had a circular window on the crew entry door on the right side of the aft fuselage and a similar window directly opposite the door on the left side. However, this arrangement was soon replaced with a larger window further forward on each side of the fuselage. At the same time, the small rectangular window just below and aft of each wing root was deleted. This later window arrangement would remain the same throughout Avenger production.

Other defining features of the TBF-1 were the single .30-caliber machine gun mounted on the top right side of the cowling and the antenna mast which was mounted at a slight rearward angle just aft of the pilot's cockpit. The rear cockpit had a seat and basic instruments, but no flight controls were provided.

Grumman produced 1,525 TBF-1s during 1942 and early 1943. As General Motors' Eastern Division began production of the Avenger, exact copies of the TBF-1 were the first 550 aircraft off the line. To differentiate between these and the Avengers built by Grumman, the designation was changed to TBM-1. Britain received 402 TBF-1 and TBM-1 Avengers, and they initially called these aircraft the Tarpon Mk I. However, this was later changed to Avenger Mk I.

A few sub-variants were produced using existing TBF-1 airframes or by modifying aircraft as they came down the production line. These included a small number of Avengers with special electronic equipment that were designated TBF-1Es. BuNo. 06031 was equipped for operations in Arctic conditions, and it received the TBF-1J designator. TBF-1P was the designation given to BuNo 06307 which carried special cameras for photo reconnais-

The aft crew entry door had a circular window on early TBF-1s. This was soon deleted, and it was replaced with a larger window just forward of the door. At the same time, the small rectangular windows were also removed from the aircraft. (Grumman)

sance work, and TBF-1Ls had a retractable searchlight in the weapons bay for nighttime illumination. Comparable aircraft built by Eastern had the same designations, except that the "F" was changed to an "M."

The TBF-1 and the TBM-1 were powered by the Wright R-2600-8 engine which provided 1,700 horse-power. Maximum speed at sea level was 251 miles-per-hour, and this rose to 271 mph at 12,000 feet. Rate of climb was 1,430 feet-per-minute, and the service ceiling was 22,400 feet. Range with a torpedo was 1,200 miles, and scouting missions of up to 1,450 miles could be performed. Empty weight was 10,080 pounds, while the maximum take-off weight was 15,900 pounds.

Above: Reports published elsewhere have stated that rocket rails were not introduced until the TBF-1C. However, the fact that TBF-1s did carry rockets is illustrated here. As with the subsequent TBF-1C, four rails could be fitted under each wing to carry 5-inch rockets. This Avenger is painted in the tri-color paint scheme which replaced the original Blue-Gray over light gray scheme. Note the white counter-shading under the wing and horizontal stabilizer. (Jones collection)

The launch officer checks under the aircraft before giving the pilot of this TBF-1 the signal to start his take-off roll. Note the two lower flaps under the cowling.
(National Archives)

The cowling of the TBF-1 had a small scoop at the top as seen in this front view. This design was continued on the TBF-1C, but all TBM-3 versions had a second scoop at the bottom of the cowling. (Grumman)

Right: In a non-standard application of the tri-color scheme, the white underneath the wings continued down to the underside of the fuselage. Note the later style forward fuselage window on this aircraft. A similar window was located in the same position on the opposite side. (National Archives)

Several defining features of the TBF-1 can be seen in this photograph. First, the antenna mast is mounted further forward than on all subsequent versions, and it was angled slightly aft. The single .30-caliber cowl gun is visible along with the indention in the cowl flap just forward of it. The second cockpit is occupied by a crewman, but in all later variants that served with the U. S. Navy, the seat was removed and replaced with radio gear. (Jones collection)

At left is the .30-caliber machine gun installation that was located on the right side of the cowling. At right is the ammunition box that was installed from the left side. This single .30-caliber weapon proved to be woefully inadequate, and it was replaced by two wing-mounted .50-caliber machine guns in all subsequent variants. (Both Grumman)

TBF-1 & TBM-1 INTERIOR DETAILS

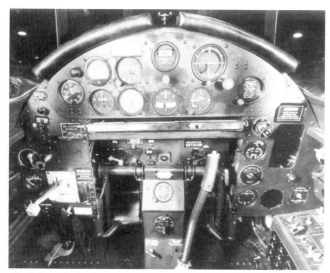

Details of the instrument panel in a TBF-1 are shown in this view. *(Grumman)*

The electrical distribution panel was the primary item on the right side of the pilot's cockpit. Controls for the radios were located above it. *(Grumman)*

The engine control quadrant and trim wheels were located on the left side of the pilot's cockpit. The cockpit interiors in Grumman-built Avengers were painted a bronze green color. The closest equivalent match in today's Federal Standard system would be 34058. All other primed areas were Interior Green which would be 34151. *(Grumman)*

This is the seat as installed in the second cockpit as seen from directly above. *(Grumman)*

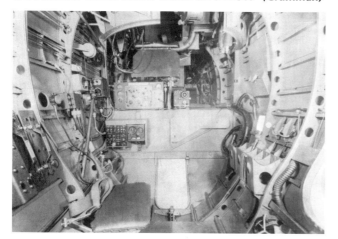

The radio compartment is shown in these two views. The photo at left looks forward revealing the radio gear and the window that looks into the bomb bay. A Norden bomb sight could be aimed through this window. Also note the configuration of the seat. This was changed to a folding seat which faced forward on subsequent versions. The two tubes in the background in the right photograph are for flares. The window in the aft entry door indicates that this is an early production TBF-1.

(Both Grumman)

TBF-1C & TBM-1C

An increase in firepower to the front was the main improvement in the TBF-1C. The single, cowl-mounted, .30-caliber machine gun was deleted, and two .50-caliber weapons were mounted in the wings just outboard of the fold. The radio mast was moved further aft on top of the canopy, and it was mounted vertically rather than being angled back. The single scoop at the top of the cowling, the single cowl flap on each side of the fuselage, and the vertical antenna mast combined to distinguish the TBF-1C from all other Avenger variants within the U. S. Navy. This TBF-1C is named "Fireball Mae" and was assigned to VT-28. It is shown here en route to Saipan during June 1944. Wartime censors have altered the stinger gun position. *(NMNA)*

Operational experience with the TBF-1 quickly revealed that the single .30-caliber machine gun mounted in the cowl was grossly inadequate. Intended primarily to supress fire from the target as the Avenger attacked, the lone .30-caliber weapon lacked the range and firepower to do the job.

The TBF-1C was developed to deal with this shortcoming. The .30-caliber cowl gun was deleted in favor of two .50-caliber machine guns mounted in the wings. These larger weapons were far more effective and provided a psycological lift for the crew as well as providing the real advantages of increased firepower and range. The one drawback, according to Don Horton, an Avenger turret gunner, was that it made some Avenger pilots believe they were flying fighters instead of torpedo bombers. As a result, overly aggressive TBF-1C pilots would sometimes try to duel Japanese fighters with less than favorable results. However, with this increased firepower to the front, the Avenger did prove more adept at engaging Japanese torpedo planes and flying boats if the situation arose.

The other noticeable external change to the TBF-1C was the relocation of the antenna mast a little further aft on the top of the canopy. In this new location, the mast was mounted vertically rather than being angled back slightly as it had been on the TBF-1. The antenna mast would remain mounted vertically in this location for all subsequent Avenger production variants. Internally, the seat was removed from the second cockpit and replaced with radio equipment. The former instrument panel in the aft cockpit gave way to the transmitter-receiver for the radio altimeter. Black boxes for the IFF system were mounted directly below it on the floor.

Production of the TBF-1C began in 1943, and a total of 764 were delivered to the U. S. Navy and Marines. Eastern built 2,332 TBM-1Cs which could be distinguished from their Grumman counterparts only by their Bureau numbers. The Fleet Air Arm received 334 of this type which it designated Tarpon Mk II and later Avenger Mk II. However, unlike the U. S. Navy, the British retained the seat and instruments in the second cockpit as they would on all of their Avengers.

The addition of the .50-caliber guns and their ammunition, along with the other minor physical changes, resulted in an increase in empty weight of about 500 pounds. Because the TBF/M-1C used the same R-2600-8 powerplant as the TBF/M-1, the additional weight resulted in a small decrease in performance. Maximum speed fell to 242 miles-per-hour at sea level and 257 mph at 12,000 feet.

Several TBM-1CPs were modified to perform photographic reconnaissance, and a few were assigned to carriers. However, most photo Avengers that served with the fleet were converted from later TBM-3 airframes.

.50-CALIBER, WING-MOUNTED, MACHINE GUNS

The .50-caliber machine guns were mounted just outboard of the wing fold on each wing, while the ammunition boxes were located further out on the wings. (Grumman)

The right machine gun is shown here from behind. Note the chute that fed ammunition to the gun. (Grumman)

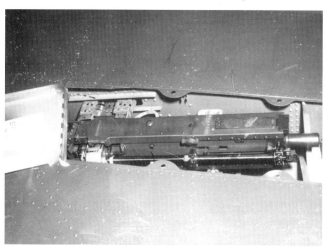

Here is the right gun as viewed from the left and looking outboard. (Grumman)

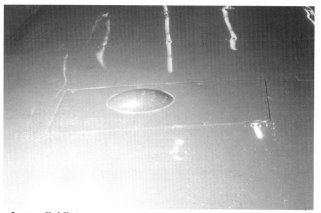

A small blister on the access door above the gun was necessary for clearance.

Ammunition could be loaded with the wing in the folded position through the use of a ladder. (National Archives)

The muzzle on each gun was well inside the wing. A blast tube extended forward from the muzzle to the leading edge of the wing.

TBF-1C & TBM-1C INTERIOR DETAILS

The pilot's cockpit in the TBF-1C differed little from that in the previous TBF-1. As far as the instrument panel was concerned, the small differences were concentrated on the right side. TBF-1Cs were built by Grumman, and had the same bronze green cockpit interiors as the TBF-1. Eastern's TBM-1Cs had cockpits that were painted Interior Green.   (Grumman)

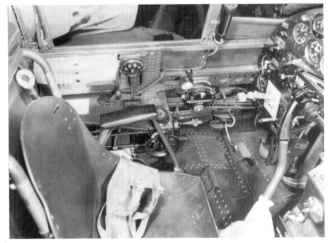

The left side of the pilot's cockpit in the TBF-1C was essentially the same as that in the TBF-1.   (Grumman)

A noticeable feature on the right side of the TBF-1C's cockpit was the port through which a flare pistol could be fired. Clips for flares can be seen in the upper corner at the rear of the cockpit.   (Grumman)

Major changes were made in the TBF-1C's aft cockpit. The instrument panel was removed, and the transmitter-receiver for the APN-1 radio altimeter was mounted in its place. This would remain standard for all subsequent U. S. Navy Avengers.   (Grumman)

The seat was also removed from the second cockpit. A framework was built into the left side of the cockpit, and the ARB radio receiver was mounted on this framework. This view looks to the left in the aft cockpit. However, British Tarpon Mk IIs, the Royal Navy's equivalent to the TBF-1C, retained the original aft cockpit with the seat in this location.   (Grumman)

Above and right: With the seat in the aft cockpit removed, the seat in the radio compartment was changed. The sideways-facing seat in the TBF-1 was replaced with a fold-down seat that placed the radio operator within easy access of much of his equipment. In the photo above, the seat is shown in the stowed or folded position. At right, the same seat is locked down and ready for use.
(Both Grumman)

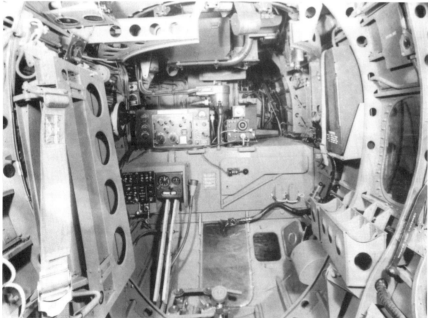

Radio equipment can be seen mounted just below the turret in this photograph that looks forward in the aft fuselage compartment. *(Grumman)*

The aft end of the radio compartment is shown here. *(Grumman)*

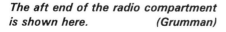

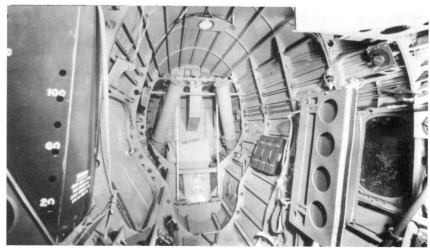

TBF-1D & TBM-1D

The TBF-1D was the first dedicated night Avenger. All TBF-1Ds were converted from existing airframes with both TBF-1s (left photo) and TBF-1Cs (right photo) being modified for this role. Armament, including the turret gun, was usually deleted in order to save weight and allow more fuel to be carried. *(Grumman)*

Although the TBF/M-1 and TBF/M-1C had the ABS radar and its associated YAGI antennas, the TBF-1D was developed as a night bomber version of the Avenger. The YAGI antennas were usually retained, although they were sometimes moved to the top of the wings.

All TBF-1Ds, and their counterpart TBM-1Ds, were converted from existing airframes with both TBF/M-1s and TBF/M-1Cs being used for the modification. An ASD-1 radar was housed in a pod which was mounted on the leading edge of the right wing. In order to save weight, the gun armament was sometimes removed totally or at least in part.

Two of the eight Avengers assigned to VC-51 aboard the USS SAN JACINTO, CVL-30, in June 1944 were TBF-1Ds. In the same month, three TBF-1Ds were among the eighteen Avengers assigned to VT-14 aboard the USS WASP, CV-18. But it was VT(N)-41, which was assigned to the USS INDEPENDENCE, CVL-22, that became the first true night bomber Avenger squadron in October 1944. Although used more often in daylight hours, this unit began to develop tactics and doctrine that would be used in night carrier operations.

A careful study of this photograph will reveal that the YAGI antennas have been moved to the top of the wings. This was done on some TBF-1Ds but by no means all. Others had their YAGI antennas removed. *(Grumman)*

"Hedy," a TBF-1D from VT(N)-41, is about to be launched from the USS INDEPENDENCE, CVL-22. This was the first operational night Avenger unit. This photo provides a good look at the radome mounted on the right wing. *(NMNA)*

TBM-3

"Georgia Peach" was a TBM-3 assigned to VT-83 and the USS ESSEX, CV-9. Because the TBM-3 was fitted with the R-2600-20 engine with two hundred more horsepower than the -8 used in earlier Avengers, additional cowl flaps had to be added to provide extra cooling. A second air scoop was added to the base of the cowling, and this supplied air to the oil cooler. Four zero-length rocket stubs were standard under each wing, thus eliminating the need for the launch rails used on earlier versions. *(NMNA)*

Although the TBF/M-1C adequately solved the problem of insufficient firepower to the front, it failed to address another shortcoming experienced in early Avenger operations. In fact, its extra weight only made it worse. The Wright R-2600-8 engine produced 1,700 horsepower, and this was marginal at best for the large heavy aircraft. Fully loaded, Avengers often struggled into the air as they launched from carriers, and they could settle badly before building up enough speed to begin gaining altitude. At times, pilots had to quickly release a bomb to reduce weight in order to prevent going for a swim.

Grumman was aware of this deficiency and studied the possibility of using the Pratt & Whitney R-2800 which provided 2,000 horsepower. However, the total production of the R-2800 went to the higher priority fighters including the Hellcat, Corsair, and Thunderbolt.

With the R-2800 eliminated as a possibility, Wright began to develop more powerful versions of the R-2600.

TBF-1, BuNo. 00393, was modified to serve as the XTBF-2 prototype. This aircraft was fitted with an R-2600-10, and it first flew on May 1, 1942. Two other TBF-1s, BuNos. 24141 and 24341, became XTBF-3 prototypes after R-2600-20 engines were installed in them. Both the -10 and the -20 versions of the Wright R-2600 produced 1,900 horsepower, and this was an increase of 200 horsepower over the R-2600-8 used in the TBF/M-1 and -1C. This was only 100 horsepower short of what the Pratt & Whitney R-2800 could produce, and more importantly, Wright could provide enough engines for the Avenger production at Eastern.

No production of the TBF/M-2 was ordered, but after building four XTBM-3 prototypes, Eastern proceeded with the TBM-3. This would become the most numerous of all Avenger variants in spite of the fact that Grumman bowed out of the Avenger picture at this time. All -3s, as well as the subsequent TBM-3E, were built by Eastern.

"DoT" was a TBM-3 which operated from the USS SUWANEE (CVE-27) as part of CVG-40. This photograph is dated March 1945. *(NMNA)*

TBM-3 DETAIL DIFFERENCES

The additional cowl flaps used on the TBM-3 can be seen in this photograph of an Avenger from VT-80 aboard the USS TICONDEROGA (CV-14). "Round Trip" lived up to its name in spite of flak damage just forward of the cockpit, and it returned ENS C. V. Higman and his crew safely back to the ship on November 11, 1944. (USNA via NMNA)

The external physical differences in the TBM-3 included two which were a direct result of the change to the more powerful R-2600-20 engine. Extra cowl flaps were added to increase cooling, and an oil cooler scoop appeared at the bottom of the cowl lip. The other major external change was the addition of four sets of zero-length rocket stubs under each wing. This eliminated the need for the large launch rails used on the earlier variants. Inside the cockpit, the instrument panel was enlarged and was a different shape, being flat across the top.

Sub-variants of the TBM-3 included the TBM-3P photo-reconnaissance version, the TBM-3J which was equipped for Arctic operations, the TBM-3L with a retractable searchlight, and the TBM-3H which was fitted with a special radar. The British called their TBM-3s, and subsequent TBM-3Es, Avenger Mk IIIs. But as with all British Avengers, these aircraft retained the seat and instruments in the aft cockpit.

The empty weight of the TBM-3 increased to 10,843 pounds, and the maximum take-off weight was 16,761 pounds. This extra weight actually negated the increased power of the -20 engine, and therefore the performance figures were approximately the same as the original TBF-1.

The oil cooler intake is clearly visible at the bottom of the cowling in the photo at left. At right is an R-2600-20 engine ready for installation on a TBM-3. (Both Eastern)

TBM-3 COCKPIT DETAILS

The instrument panel in the TBM-3 was changed significantly from that used in earlier variants. It was flatter across the top, and the layout of instruments was different. Lighting in the cockpit was changed to improve night flying. Because all TBM-3s were built by Eastern, Interior Green was used as the base color.　　(Eastern)

Only detail changes were made on the left side of the cockpit when compared to the earlier variants. (Eastern)

Although the electric distribution panel remained the major item on the right side of the cockpit, numerous changes can be seen with respect to the radio gear. The small box near the top of the photograph is the ARC-1 control, while directly below it is the ARC-5 control. Moving aft at the same level are the ARB receiver control, the APX-2 control, and the ARB remote tuner.　　(Eastern)

Among the items on the right auxiliary panel are the oxygen flow indicator, unit engine gage, accelerometer, clock, fuel quantity indicator, and the charger for the wing guns.　　(Eastern)

TBM-3D

A few TBM-3s were modified to TBM-3D night bombers in much the same way that TBF-1s and TBF-1Cs had been converted to TBF-1Ds. The same radome was mounted on the right wing, and the YAGI antennas were relocated to the top of each wing.

(Eastern)

The addition of the ASD-1 radar to existing TBM-3 airframes resulted in the TBM-3D night bomber variant in the same manner that the TBF/M-1D had been previously converted from TBF/M-1 and TBF/M-1C airframes (see page 22). The radome was again mounted on the leading edge of the right wing, and the main scope was located in the radio compartment. The pilot also had a smaller scope in his cockpit.

VT(N)-90 was commissioned in August 1944, and it embarked in the USS ENTERPRISE, CV-6, with twenty-seven TBM-3Ds in January 1945. By this time, the ENTERPRISE had been designated as a night carrier, and VT(N)-90 was part of Air Group 90(N) which was specially formed for night operations. In addition to the TBM-3Ds, this air group also included VF(N)-90, a night fighter squadron with nineteen F6F-5N night fighters and eleven F6F-5 standard Hellcats. VS-90 was also added to this air group in late February or early March, and it operated twenty-one TBM-3E Avengers with their APS-4 radars.

With this unusual air group aboard, ENTERPRISE joined Task Force 58 in March 1945, but it remained operational for only a few weeks. On April 13, 1945, a kamikaze plunged through the Big E's flight deck and knocked her out of action for the remainder of the war.

In February 1945, five TBM-3Ds were assigned to VT(N)-41 in USS INDEPENDENCE, CVL-22, replacing the four TBF/M-1Ds in that unit. USS SARATOGA, CV-3, was the other night carrier to see action. VT(N)-53, with seventeen TBM-3Ds, was part of Air Group 53 aboard SARA during the closing months of the war.

As with the TBF/M-1D, the machine gun armament and most of the armor plate in many TBM-3Ds was removed to save weight. In some cases the entire turret was taken out. Operating at night reduced the threat from Japanese fighters, and the increased performance from the lighter aircraft was more desirable. This weight savings also permitted additional fuel and ordnance to be carried.

A searchlight could be mounted under the left wing for night search operations. Using the light in close proximity to the enemy was unwise, because it indicated exactly where the aircraft was in the night sky. *(Eastern)*

This rear view provides a different look at the radome and the two YAGI antennas mounted on top of the wings. *(Eastern)*

TBM-3E

"Satan's Helper" was a TBM-3E assigned to VT-83 and the USS ESSEX, CV-9, during the final months of the war. The tunnel gun was deleted from the -3E, but the radio man was kept busy operating the APS-4 radar. The white radome for the radar can be seen under the right wing. The scope and controls were located in the aft fuselage compartment. Note that this particular TBM-3E has the internal tail hook. (Madden via NMNA)

Wright has squeezed every ounce of horsepower out of the R-2600 engine, so with no Pratt & Whitney R-2800s available, the only way to improve performance in the Avenger was to reduce weight. This resulted in the TBM-3E variant which had an empty weight of some 300 pounds less than a TBM-3. But more importantly, the loaded weight of 14,160 pounds was 2,600 pounds less than that of the TBM-3. Most noticeable of these weight-saving measures was the deletion of the stinger gun in the radio compartment.

Several sources state that the TBM-3E had an external tail hook. But the fact is that more TBM-3Es had the standard internal hook than the later external arresting hook. The change to the external hook was not made until BuNo. 86175, which was well into the TBM-3E production. Corrosion problems with the internal hook

had resulted in a number of failures, and this necessitated the change to the external hook. Overall length was increased by 11.5 inches with the external hook, because it extended beyond the trailing edge of the rudder. The same change was also made during the production of SB2C-4E Helldivers.

The TBM-3E was fitted with an APS-4 radar which was noticeable because of the white radome carried under the right wing. The scope and some of the controls were located on the right side of the radio compartment just forward of the entry door. The rest of the associated equipment was mounted in the center fuselage compartment. The drawing on page 29 illustrates where each component was positioned in the aircraft.

The Royal Navy received 222 Avenger Mk IIIs which included a mix of both TBM-3s and TBM-3Es.

Late production TBM-3Es like this one were fitted with external tail hooks. This Avenger is shown aboard the USS LEYTE, CV-32, in the post-war markings of FASRON 6. Although this photograph was taken in May 1952, the aircraft is still serving in its original bomber role. Many other TBM-3Es were converted for other specialized missions and served into the early 1950s with the U. S. Navy. Still others remained in operation even longer with the air forces and navies of other nations. (Brown via NMNA)

APS-4 RADAR

The radome for the APS-4 and its mount are shown here from behind. The radome was carried just outboard of the zero-length rocket launchers.
(National Archives)

The scope and controls for the APS-4 were located in the aft fuselage compartment. They were mounted next to the forward window on the right side. (National Archives)

The APS-4 scope and controls are shown here from a different angle that reveals additional details of the equipment. But this gear, along with the radome, was only a portion of the APS-4 system. See the following page for a look at the entire system and where each component was located inside the aircraft. (National Archives)

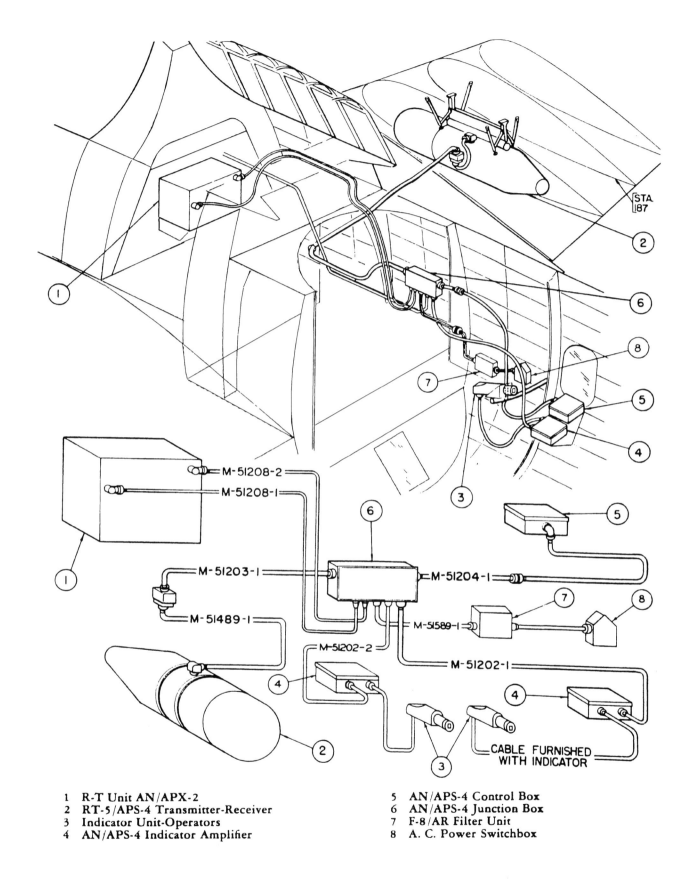

1	R-T Unit AN/APX-2	5	AN/APS-4 Control Box
2	RT-5/APS-4 Transmitter-Receiver	6	AN/APS-4 Junction Box
3	Indicator Unit-Operators	7	F-8/AR Filter Unit
4	AN/APS-4 Indicator Amplifier	8	A. C. Power Switchbox

Taken from the erection and maintenance manual, this drawing illustrates the components of the APS-4 radar system and indicates where they were located inside the TBM-3E.

(U. S. Navy via Gallo)

TBM-3E DETAIL DIFFERENCES

Above left and right: The cowl flaps on the TBM-3E were slightly revised from what had been used on the TBM-3. The lower flaps on each side were not indented as they had been on the TBM-3.

The actuators for the cowl flaps can be seen in this view along with the exhaust piping on the right side of the engine.

The tunnel gun was deleted from the TBM-3E, and the position was covered over with sheet metal.

POST-WAR AVENGERS

The TBM-3W was fitted with an APS-20 surface search radar beneath the fuselage. The large radome occupied almost the entire space between the two main landing gear struts. Auxiliary tail fins were added to the horizontal stabilizers.
(NMNA)

From the very beginning of carrier operations in the U. S. Navy, scouting planes extended the eyes of the fleet far beyond the horizons that were visible from the tallest mast. Indeed, these aircraft could range much further than the shipboard radars that began to sprout from the masts about the time World War II began.

Scouts not only flew missions searching for the enemy, they also warned of his approach. But even after surface and air search radars became standard on ships, the scouting planes still relied on visual sightings by the pilot or a crewman in the aircraft. Therefore, poor weather and the darkness of night reduced their effective-

ness considerably. The idea of installing a search radar in an aircraft promised considerable improvement in detection during the day or night as well as in bad weather.

In early 1942, even before the Avenger became operational, the Navy asked the Massachusetts Institute of Technology to develop an airborne radar which could be carried beneath the fuselage of the aircraft. Produced under the name *Project Cadillac*, the APS-20 was designed to fit in Avenger's weapons bay. The eight-foot wide antenna was installed in a large radome which was as wide as the main landing gear would allow. The turret was removed from the aircraft to make room for associ-

Being among the largest aircraft to operate from carriers, the Avenger was the logical choice for the first onboard cargo plane to be used by the U. S. Navy. The concept became known as COD, for Carrier Onboard Delivery. Avengers modified to serve as cargo aircraft received the designation TBM-3R. Seven passengers could also be transported between carriers and the shore. This -3R was assigned to VR-23, and it operated from Yodo Island during 1953.   *(NMNA)*

TBM-3Ns were converted to provide night attack capabilities that were better than those of the TBM-3D. The TBM-3N in the photograph at left was assigned to VCN-2 at Key West NAS, Florida, during 1948. At right is a close-up of the modified canopy with the radar operator located in the former turret position. *(Both NMNA)*

ated equipment and two operators. The lower fuselage was redesigned from the radome aft in order to provide more ground clearance, and two auxiliary tail fins were added to the horizontal stabilizer to increase directional stability. Designated the XTBM-3W, the prototype first flew on August 5, 1944. Conversion of existing TBM-3 and TBM-3E airframes to TBM-3Ws began almost immediately. Crew training began in early 1945, but Japan surrendered before the first TBM-3Ws could be deployed to the fleet.

Although the end of the war caused the Navy to cancel further Avenger production, the value of the TBM-3W was clearly established, and the first deployment to the fleet occurred in mid-1946.

The primary use of the TBM-3W, and the subsequent TBM-3W-2, saw it teamed with another Avenger conversion, the TBM-3S, in anti-submarine operations. Using its APS-20 radar, the TBM-3W "hunter" would provide target information to the TBM 3S "killer," which was specially equipped and armed to destroy submarines. Improved "killers" were designated TBM-3S-2.

Although some Avengers served during the post-war years in their originally intended bomber role, many more were modified to perform other specific missions. Another version with a search radar was the TBM-3H. The TBM-3N was specially equipped for night attack missions, thus replacing the TBM-3D. The TBM-3Q was an electronic countermeasures aircraft intended to jam enemy radars. The TBM-3R became the first carrier onboard delivery aircraft transporting personnel and equipment between the ships and shore installations.

Still other Avengers were found in non-combat operations. The TBM-3M was used in missile test programs, and TBM-3Us could be found on many Naval Air stations serving as utility or hack aircraft.

Many surplus Avengers were sold to other nations where they served as bombers and in specialized roles after being modified. Even Japan, the country the Avenger had helped defeat, operated twenty Avengers in the mid-1950s.

Even after the Avenger was retired from U. S. military service in 1954, many could be found in civilian service fighting forest fires. Other nations retained them in military use well into the 1960s.

Colorful TBM-3Us served as utility aircraft in a variety of roles. Some were hacks, while others towed targets. The wings, main landing gear, horizontal tails, and vertical stabilizer on this aircraft are painted gloss yellow. The rudder and the bands on the wings are red-orange. This TBM-3U was assigned to VX-1 at Boca Chica during 1948. (I. F. Brown via NMNA)

AVENGER DETAILS IN COLOR

WRIGHT R-2600 ENGINE

Avengers were powered by the Wright R-2600 radial engine. The R-2600-8, with 1,700 horsepower, was used in the TBF/M-1 and TBF/M-1C, while the R-2600-20, rated at 1,900 horsepower, was fitted in the TBM-3 and TBM-3E. This R-2600 is on display at the Museum of Aviation at Warner Robins, Georgia.

The distribution ring was a natural chrome metal, and the crankcase was painted a medium gray. This is what a new engine would have looked like just after being installed in the aircraft.

Features on the rear of the engine can be studied in this view.

A Hamilton-Standard propeller was used on all Avenger variants. This close-up of one of the blades shows the markings which include the manufacturer's logo.

Details of the propeller hub can be seen here. Note the yellow line-up mark. The natural metal manufacturer's plates are visible on the crankcase housing.

TBM-3E COCKPIT COLORS & DETAILS

This Avenger has a cockpit which has been faithfully restored to specifications for a TBM-3E. Only one radio-navigation instrument has been added on the panel to allow the aircraft to be flown today. It is the second instrument from the right on the second row down from the top of the main panel. This instrument replaced the standard APN-1 limit switch. Otherwise, the colors and features are as they would have been on an operational TBM-3E. Note the gun sight above the panel and the compass at the top of the windscreen.

The control column and center console are visible here. Note the canvas boot on the control column. The interiors of Eastern-built Avengers were painted Interior Green.

The throttle quadrant was the main feature on the left side of the cockpit. Trim wheels are mounted further aft. The case for the maps and records is on the side wall just above the armrest. The black box, which is just visible in the lower right corner, was added to hold the modern transponders, and it replaces the mount for the pilot's radar scope in a vintage aircraft. Otherwise, this photograph is accurate for a wartime TBM-3E.

The large electrical distribution panel takes up most of the cockpit's right side. The black boxes just above it are (from left to right) the ARC-5 control, ATC transmitter control, ARB receiver control, and the APX-2 control. Above the armrest is the ARB remote tuner, and just below it is the port through which flares could be fired. The flares were carried in the natural metal clips on the aft cockpit wall. Attached to the forward brace on the armrest is the intercom switch.

The two straps of the shoulder harness and the thicker lap belts can be seen in this photograph of the pilot's seat. The seat itself was simply a metal bucket with a tubular frame, and the pilot's parachute acted as a bottom cushion to sit on. Armrests were fitted on each side to help reduce fatigue on long flights.

The transmitter-receiver unit for the APN-1 radio altimeter was located in the aft cockpit. This area was used for basic instruments in the XTBF-1 and the TBF-1 (see page 13), but on all subsequent production variants, this APN-1 gear was located here. Note how the wooden antenna mast extends down into the cockpit.

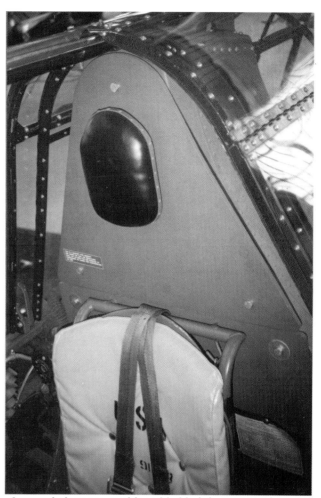

Armor plating was positioned behind the seat, and a small cushioned headrest was attached at its center.

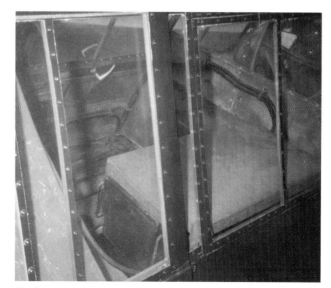

Radio gear replaced the second seat used in the TBF-1, and the ARB receiver was located in this position on the left side of the cockpit. During flight, access to this area could be gained from the aft compartment through a crawlway on the right side of the aircraft. This photograph was taken from the left wing and looks aft into the second cockpit in a TBM-3E. An interior view of similar equipment in a TBF-1C can be found on page 20.

TURRET DETAILS & COLORS

Oxygen for the turret gunner was supplied through a hose next to the seat back.

A gun camera was mounted near the top of the turret. Below it was the contour follower and the gun sight. Spent shells were jettisoned down the natural metal chute on this side of the gun.

Details of the turret control unit are shown here. An iron ring and bead sight is mounted just above it. To the right of the control handle is the oxygen blinker. The gun was fired by a trigger on the control handle.

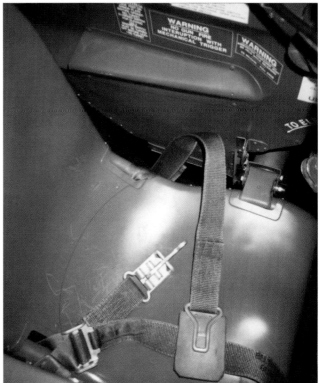

The base of the gunner's seat and the rather thin seat belts can be seen here. Note the built-in arm rest next to the seat.

Various plates and decals next to the gunner's seat are shown here. These accurately represent what was in the turret when it was originally produced.

This photograph was taken from inside the aft compartment, and it looks up and forward into the gunner's chair. The lower plate with the WARNING stencil could be folded up out of the way when the turret was not occupied.

The lower part of the structural components between the turret and the aft end of the canopy assembly is revealed in this photograph.

On the original version of the Grumman turret, cutout gear prevented the gunner from inadvertently firing into his own aircraft. On the later version of the turret, the interrupter gear shown here replaced the earlier system. It was mounted on the turret azimuth ring and rotated with the turret assembly.

The upper part of the assembly between the turret and the aft canopy is illustrated in this view.

RADIO OPERATOR'S COMPARTMENT

This view of the forward left corner of the aft compartment shows the intervalometer near the lower center of the photograph. The silver box above it is the station distributor. The oxygen blinker is visible near the center of the photo, and just above it is the turret power switch.

A switch box, tool kit, and a can of drinking water are mounted just forward of the larger window on the right side of the aircraft. When the APS-4 radar equipment was fitted, the scope and some of the other smaller equipment were located in this position as illustrated on pages 28 and 29.

The main radio transmitter is the large black box just below the turret. The relief tube for the turret gunner and radio operator can be seen just below it.

Details on the left side of the aft compartment are shown here. Note the oxygen hose for the radio operator.

The engine starter crank was stored just below the crew entry door.

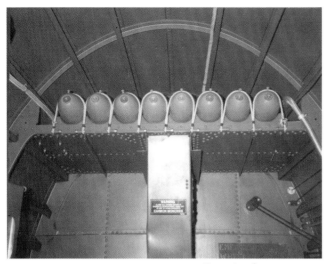

Aircraft float lights, which were small marker buoys, were stored at the top of the aft compartment at the rear.

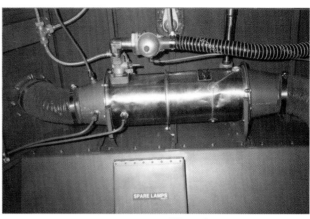

Late in the Avenger's service life, a heater was mounted laterally across the top of the rear compartment. Air was brought in through a scoop on the spine of the fuselage, heated, then discharged into the compartment. This view looks straight up at the center of the compartment.

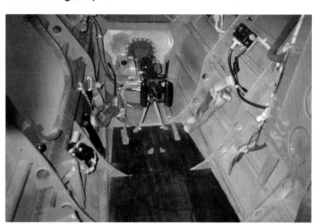

The stinger gun can be seen here. Although the gun and mount are accurate, it should be noted that this gun was not operationally mounted in a TBM-3E. However, it has been added to this restored aircraft. This means that the triangular-shaped side windows are missing, and the shape of the aft window is slightly different. This photograph is included to provide a reference for the correct colors. See page 52 for more photographs of the stinger gun position in an operational aircraft.

The radio operator's seat could be folded up and stowed against the left side of the fuselage as shown in the photo at left. When in use, it locked down in position, as seen at right, and the seat back folded upward. Cushions were usually placed in the seat.

WEAPONS BAY DETAILS & COLORS

Batteries were located at the forward end of the bomb bay. The interior of the vent flap for the oil cooler can be seen just forward of the bomb bay.

Almost the entire length of the bomb bay's interior can be seen in this photograph. The interior was painted Interior Green.

The small windows at the aft end of the weapons bay were on most Avengers, but they were deleted from some late production aircraft. Part of the mechanism for actuating the bomb bay doors is also visible in this photograph.

Torpedoes were moved to the aircraft on a rather simple but sturdy dolly.

This interesting photograph shows how the wooden vanes, used on some torpedoes, fit into the aft end of the weapons bay. It also reveals how the wood structure was attached to the fins on the torpedo.

AVENGER DIMENSIONS

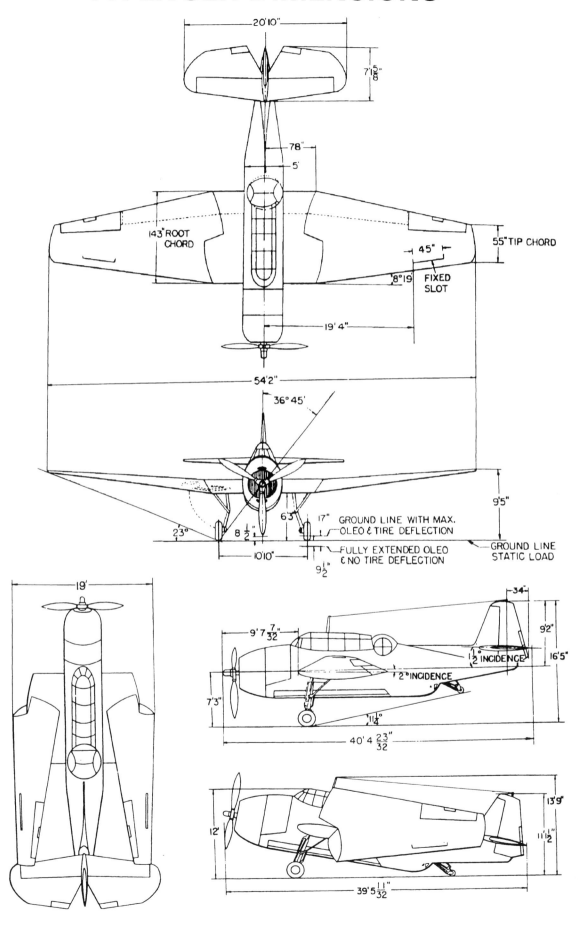

DETAIL & SCALE 1/72nd SCALE DRAWINGS

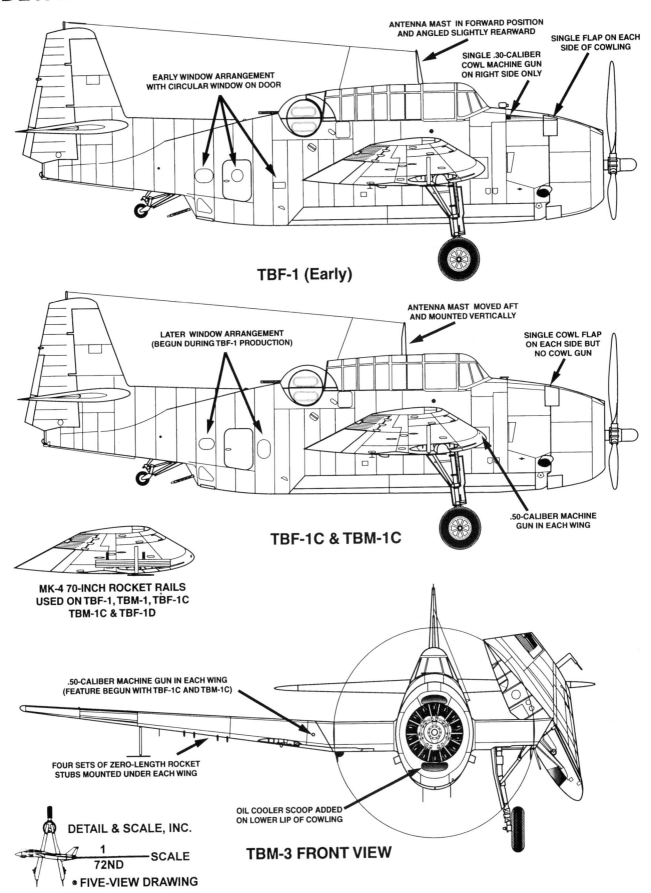

ANTENNA MAST IN FORWARD POSITION
AND ANGLED SLIGHTLY REARWARD

SINGLE .30-CALIBER
COWL MACHINE GUN
ON RIGHT SIDE ONLY

SINGLE FLAP ON EACH
SIDE OF COWLING

EARLY WINDOW ARRANGEMENT
WITH CIRCULAR WINDOW ON DOOR

TBF-1 (Early)

ANTENNA MAST MOVED AFT
AND MOUNTED VERTICALLY

SINGLE COWL FLAP
ON EACH SIDE BUT
NO COWL GUN

LATER WINDOW ARRANGEMENT
(BEGUN DURING TBF-1 PRODUCTION)

.50-CALIBER MACHINE
GUN IN EACH WING

TBF-1C & TBM-1C

MK-4 70-INCH ROCKET RAILS
USED ON TBF-1, TBM-1, TBF-1C
TBM-1C & TBF-1D

.50-CALIBER MACHINE GUN IN EACH WING
(FEATURE BEGUN WITH TBF-1C AND TBM-1C)

FOUR SETS OF ZERO-LENGTH ROCKET
STUBS MOUNTED UNDER EACH WING

OIL COOLER SCOOP ADDED
ON LOWER LIP OF COWLING

TBM-3 FRONT VIEW

DETAIL & SCALE, INC.

1
——— SCALE
72ND

● FIVE-VIEW DRAWING

DETAIL & SCALE 1/72nd SCALE COPYRIGHT © DRAWINGS BY LLOYD JONES

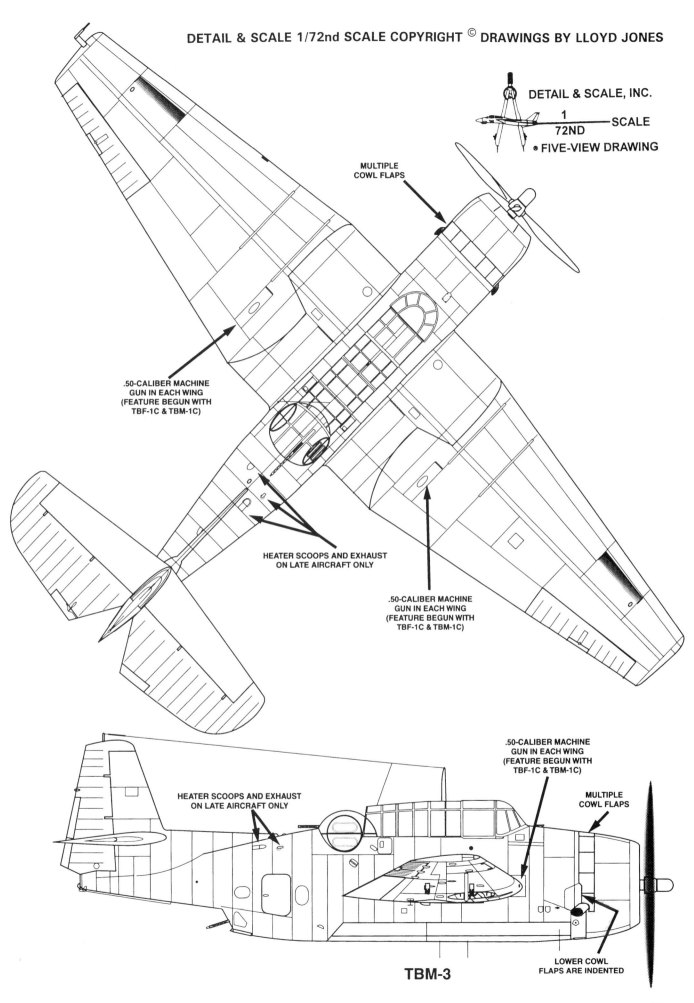

DETAIL & SCALE, INC.

1
SCALE
72ND

® FIVE-VIEW DRAWING

MULTIPLE
COWL FLAPS

.50-CALIBER MACHINE
GUN IN EACH WING
(FEATURE BEGUN WITH
TBF-1C & TBM-1C)

HEATER SCOOPS AND EXHAUST
ON LATE AIRCRAFT ONLY

.50-CALIBER MACHINE
GUN IN EACH WING
(FEATURE BEGUN WITH
TBF-1C & TBM-1C)

.50-CALIBER MACHINE
GUN IN EACH WING
(FEATURE BEGUN WITH
TBF-1C & TBM-1C)

MULTIPLE
COWL FLAPS

HEATER SCOOPS AND EXHAUST
ON LATE AIRCRAFT ONLY

LOWER COWL
FLAPS ARE INDENTED

TBM-3

43

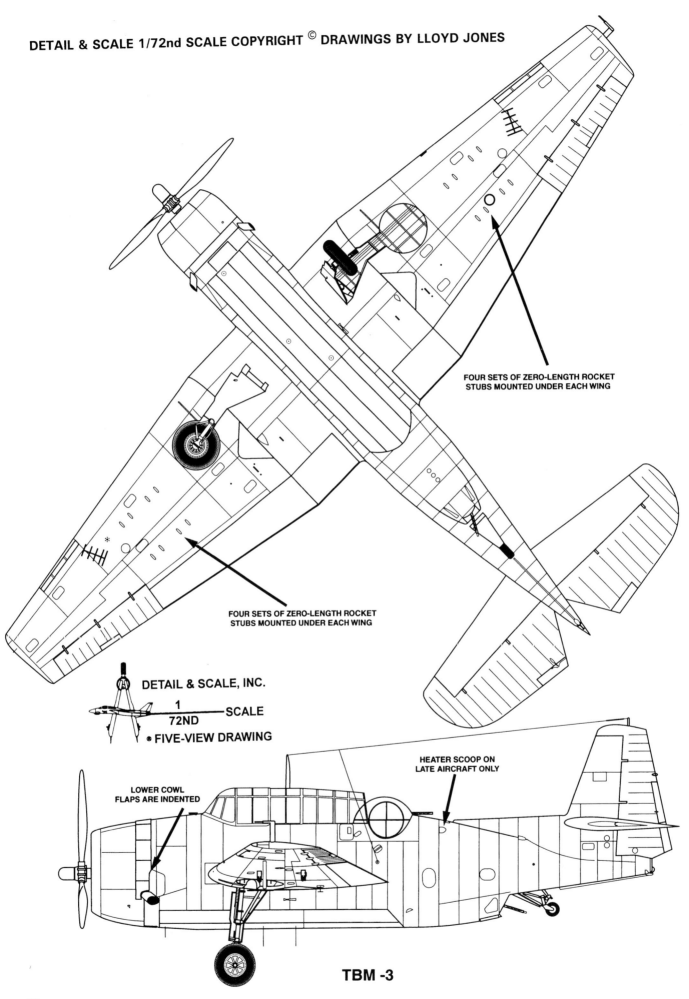

FOUR SETS OF ZERO-LENGTH ROCKET
STUBS MOUNTED UNDER EACH WING

FOUR SETS OF ZERO-LENGTH ROCKET
STUBS MOUNTED UNDER EACH WING

DETAIL & SCALE, INC.

$\dfrac{1}{72ND}$ ── SCALE

⊛ FIVE-VIEW DRAWING

HEATER SCOOP ON
LATE AIRCRAFT ONLY

LOWER COWL
FLAPS ARE INDENTED

TBM -3

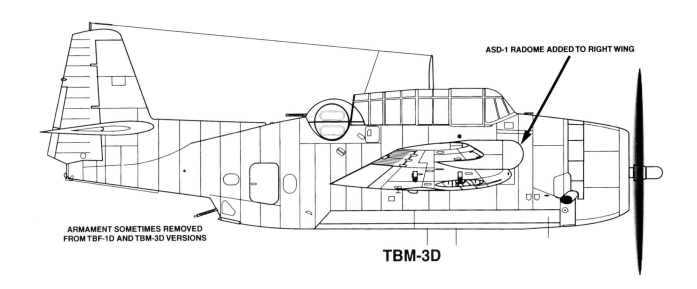

ASD-1 RADOME ADDED TO RIGHT WING

ARMAMENT SOMETIMES REMOVED
FROM TBF-1D AND TBM-3D VERSIONS

TBM-3D

TOP   BOTTOM

ASD-1 RADOME USED
ON TBF-1D AND TBM-3D

DETAIL & SCALE, INC.

$\dfrac{1}{72ND}$ —— SCALE

● FIVE-VIEW DRAWING

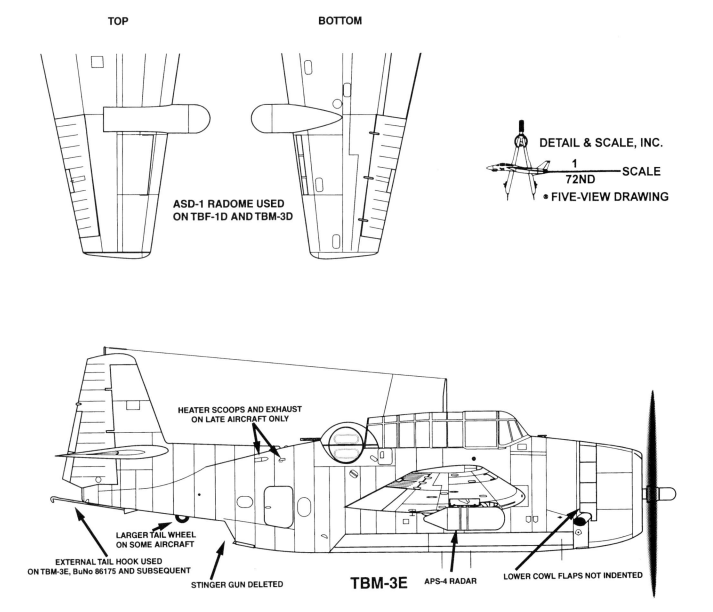

HEATER SCOOPS AND EXHAUST
ON LATE AIRCRAFT ONLY

LARGER TAIL WHEEL
ON SOME AIRCRAFT

EXTERNAL TAIL HOOK USED
ON TBM-3E, BuNo 86175 AND SUBSEQUENT

STINGER GUN DELETED

TBM-3E

APS-4 RADAR

LOWER COWL FLAPS NOT INDENTED

DETAIL & SCALE 1/72nd SCALE COPYRIGHT © DRAWINGS BY LLOYD JONES

AVENGER DETAILS

WEAPONS BAY

The forward end of both sets of bomb bay doors can be seen in these two photographs. Note the cross section of the doors as well as the actuating link.

With no ordnance loaded, the entire interior of the bomb bay can be seen in this view that looks aft. (Grumman)

The inner doors were thicker at the aft end, and there were lightening holes in the aft wall. The actuating linkage was mounted several inches forward of the trailing edge.

INTERNAL STORES

At left, cables have been attached to a torpedo in preparation for hoisting it up into the weapons bay. At right, the torpedo has been secured in place.   *(Both Grumman)*

Bombs were also raised into the bay through means of a hoist and cable system. At left, a 1000-pound bomb is ready to be raised into the bay, and at right, the bomb is shown in position.   *(Both Grumman)*

Smaller bombs were attached to racks which could be installed at several different locations along the sides of the bomb bay. At left, two of these racks can be seen attached on the right side of the bay. The racks were unpainted natural metal. At right, twelve 100-pound bombs are shown mounted to racks like these. Although 250-pound bombs were sometimes carried, 500-pound bombs were used more often. These same racks were also used to carry depth bombs on anti-submarine missions.

(Both Grumman)

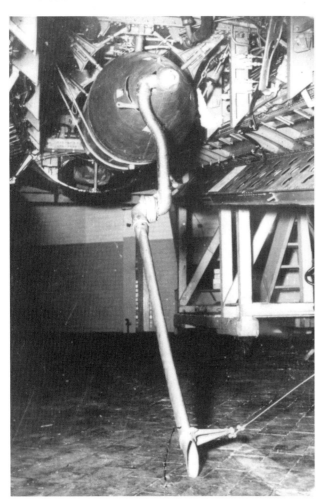

Avengers were sometimes used to lay smoke screens. The tank fit inside the forward end of the bay, and the dispensing tube extended down and aft as seen here. This view looks forward from behind the tank.

(Grumman)

To provide extra range for ferry flights or scouting missions, a fuel tank could be carried inside the weapons bay.

(Grumman)

ROCKETS

On TBF/M-1 and TBF/M-1C variants, launch rails were sometimes fitted under the wings to carry rockets. The rails were not always present, and they were usually installed only when rocket armament was required for a specific mission. Here, a TBM-1C from VT-15 makes an unassisted launch from the USS ESSEX, CV-9, with a partial load of rockets.
(Paul Madden via NMNA)

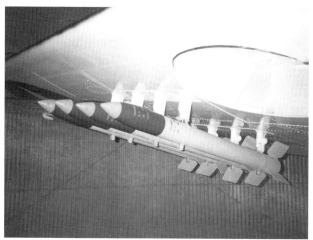 

Beginning with the TBM-3, zero-length rocket stubs were fitted as standard equipment. Four 5-inch rockets could be carried under each wing.

At left is a photo of the rocket stubs under the left wing of a TBM-3E, while at right is a close-up showing how the ignition wires attached to both the aft stubs and the rockets.

DEFENSIVE ARMAMENT

TURRET DETAILS

With the glass and framework removed, details of the original Grumman-designed turret are clearly visible. At left is the basic gun position without any additional equipment installed. At right, the armored glass and gunner's seat can be seen.
(Both Grumman)

Additional details of the turret are illustrated in these two views. *(Both Grumman)*

Although it was rather confining, the turret's enclosure provided excellent visibility aft and to the left side of the aircraft. The gun restricted visibility to the right side, so gunners often kept the turret moving in azimuth to search the sky when enemy aircraft were known to be in the area. *(Grumman)*

The gunner could make an emergency escape through a removable panel on the port side of the turret. The red handle at the center released four pins in the framework, and this allowed the panel to be jettisoned from the aircraft. This photograph shows the inside of the panel after it was removed from the turret.

This view looks up into the turret from directly below the gun. The handle on the emergency escape panel is visible at the center of the photograph.

The gunner's control handle and trigger can be seen in both of these views. Both mechanical and electrical sights were provided, and a firing interrupter prevented the gunner from inadvertently hitting his own aircraft in the heat of battle. Additional photographs of the turret can be found in the color section. *(Both Grumman)*

STINGER .30-CALIBER MACHINE GUN

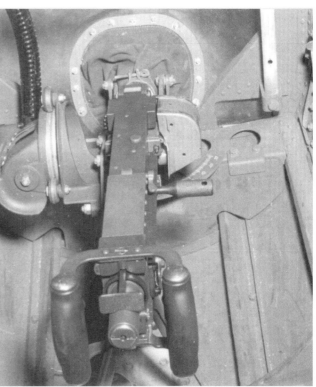

Left: A .30-caliber tunnel gun was installed in the lower aft fuselage on all Avenger variants through the TBM-3. Also called the stinger gun, it was manned by the radio operator, and it provided protection to the rear and below the aircraft. Ammunition was stored in a box mounted just above the gun on the right side of the aircraft.
(Grumman)

Above: This close-up reveals how the gun was mounted in the aircraft. *(Grumman)*

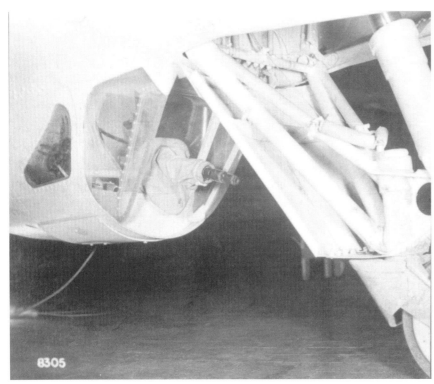

This exterior view shows the proximity of the gun to the extended tail wheel. Also note the details of the rear and side windows as well as the canvas boot that surrounds the barrel of the gun. *(Grumman)*

LANDING GEAR DETAILS

LEFT MAIN LANDING GEAR

An overall view provides a good look at the left main landing gear. In this case, a protective plate has been installed over the wheel. *(Grumman)*

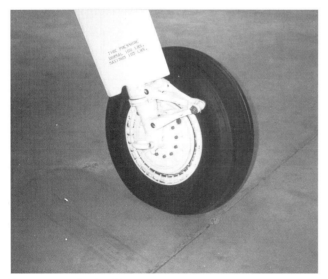

Features on the inside of the left main wheel can be seen in this photo. Note the tire pressure stenciling on the door. Tires on carrier-based aircraft were inflated to very high pressure, and they had very little "weighted" effect.

After Avengers had been in service for a year or two, it became more common to see them without the protective covers on their wheels. Details of the uncovered main gear wheel can be seen here.

The left main gear door is shown here from underneath the aircraft.

RIGHT MAIN LANDING GEAR

The slightly "bent" design of the main landing gear is evident in this front view of the right gear.

A hook for the catapult bridle was attached to each main gear strut, and it extended through the top of the gear door as shown here. Also note the two small door extensions between the top of the door and the wing. This is the right landing gear as viewed from the front.

The interior of the wheel wells were usually painted the same color as the underside of the wing. This is the outer portion of the right main gear well.

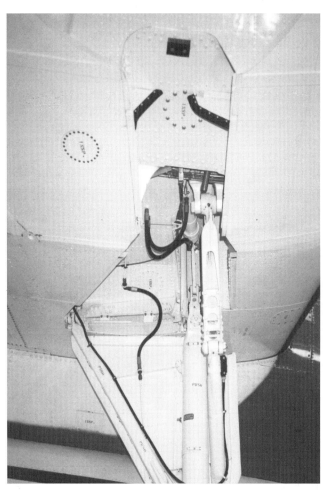

Details of the inner portion of the right main gear well are illustrated in this photograph.

TAIL LANDING GEAR

The Avenger had a retractable tail wheel mounted just aft of the stinger gun position. Both pneumatic and hard rubber tires were used on the wheel.
(Left author, right Grumman)

LANDING GEAR DRAWINGS

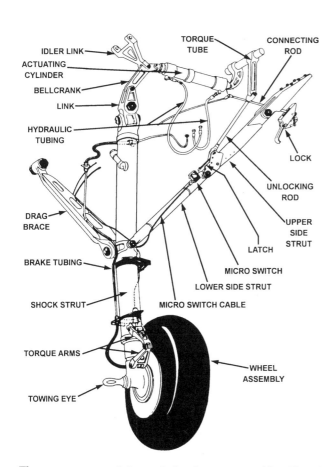
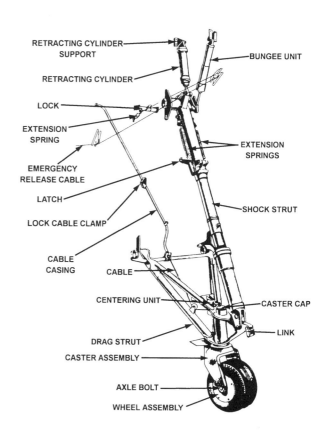

The components of the main landing gear are identified in this drawing that was taken from the maintenance manual for the Avenger. *(U. S. Navy via Gallo)*

Features of the tail wheel assembly are identified in this drawing. *(U. S. Navy via Gallo)*

CANOPY DETAILS

Access to the pilot's cockpit could be gained through sliding canopy panels on both sides. But the aft cockpit could only be entered on the right side as shown here. The right side and top panels hinged up to this open position. This arrangement remained even after the seat was deleted on the TBF-1C and all subsequent American variants.

Details of the windscreen are visible in this view.

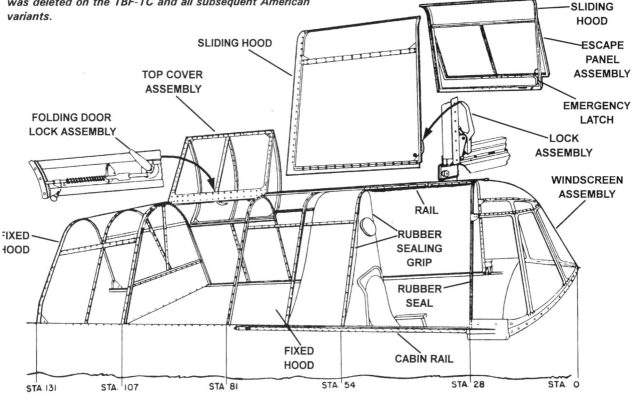

The various features of the canopy are identified in this detailed drawing which has been adapted from a similar drawing in the maintenance manual for the Avenger.

(U. S. Navy via Gallo)

FUSELAGE DETAILS

A mount for a combat camera was located just forward of the windscreen. The camera is shown in position in this view, but more often than not, it was not installed on the aircraft.

On the right side of the fuselage next to the pilot's cockpit was a port through which signal flares could be fired. A grounding point was below and slightly aft of this port.

A tube ran laterally through the fuselage just forward of the turret. Life rafts and survival gear were stored inside the tube which could be accessed from either side of the aircraft. The panel on the left side has been removed in this photograph, and the yellow raft is visible inside.

The right exhaust is the prominent feature in this photo. Just below it is a red button with an unusual marking around it. This is where the starter crank was inserted. The starter engage handle is located just aft of the exhaust. Further aft are the A. C. power connection and the battery plug.

Under the nose section was the exhaust flap for the oil cooler. The small tube that is cut off at an angle is the crankcase vent.

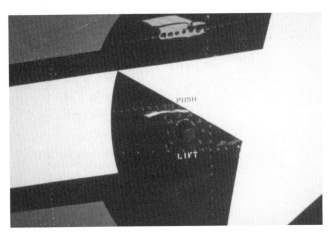

A lift tube ran completely through the aft fuselage. It is within the blue area of the national insignia, and the word LIFT is stencilled just below it in white.

On the spine of the aircraft, and just aft of the turret, was a clear position light. The covered vent was the exhaust for the heater in the aft compartment. The tubular intake provided air for the element inside the heater. These last two features were only on aircraft which had the heater added in the rear compartment.

On some aircraft a scoop was located on the left side of the aft fuselage. Air was routed from this scoop into the heater where it was warmed for crew comfort in the aft compartment. These heaters were added to TBM-3s and -3Es late in the war, and they were not on all aircraft.

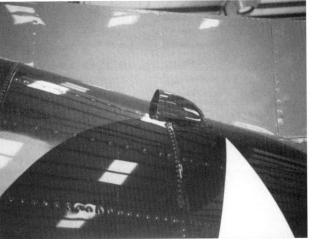

Further aft was another scoop which provided positive pressure in the aft compartment. This scoop was on all aircraft.

The tapered rod antenna on the left bomb bay door was for the IFF system. A second rod antenna for the IFF system was mounted at the front of the outer right bomb bay door.

Later Avengers had a venturi tube on the left side of the fuselage below the wing. Just aft of it is a drain which appears to be a black dot in this photo. Directly below the drain is the angled drain for the pilot's relief tube.

Left and above: On each side of the fuselage, and just aft of the trailing edge of the wing, was a step and a hand hold. The step was covered by a spring-loaded door. These enabled both flight and ground crew personnel easy access to the walkways on the top of each wing. The photo above also provides a good look at the windows as installed on all U. S. Avengers except for very early production TBF-1s.

Left and above: The radio operator and turret gunner boarded the aircraft through a door in the aft right side of the fuselage. Doors on early TBF-1s had a circular window, but this was soon deleted on production lines in favor of an oval window located just forward of the door. At left is an exterior look at the door in the closed position. Details on the inside of the door are illustrated in the photograph above.

WING DETAILS

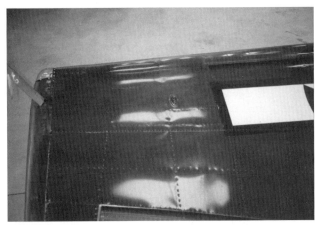

This top view of the left wing tip shows the navigation light just forward of the pitot probe and the small blue formation light just outboard of the national insignia. Part of the "mail box" slot can be seen forward of the bar on the national insignia.

The large L-shaped pitot probe was mounted at an angle on the left wing tip.

Navigation lights were located at the forward edge of each wing tip. They were clear, and there was an element of the appropriate color located inside. This is the navigation light on the right wing tip as seen from below.

Fuel tanks were filled from a point on top of each wing near the root. The caps were painted red. This is the fueling point for the left wing tank, and the one for the right tank would be in the same location on the right wing.

A black, non-skid walkway was on top of each wing at the root. However, it did not extend all the way to the leading edge of the wing.

The aileron hinge brackets were just like those used on the Hellcat.

The ailerons were made of fabric, and each had a metal trim tab controlled by an actuating rod on the top. This is the trim tab on top of the left aileron.

"Mail box" anti-stall slots were built into the leading edge of each wing. This is the slot on the right wing as seen from below.

External stores could be carried on a rack mounted under each wing. This is where the APS-4 pod was carried under the right wing of TBM-3Es.   (Eastern)

To extend range, while leaving the bomb bay available to carry weapons, external fuel tanks could be attached to the fixed portion of each wing. Each tank had a capacity of fifty-eight gallons. Note the closed triangular-shaped door in each photograph. This hinged door hung vertically when the wings were folded. The inverted "T" shaped device seen in each photo is an APN-1 radio altimeter antenna. There was an identical antenna in the same place under the right wing.

(Both Grumman)

Moveable YAGI radar antennas were usually mounted under each wing on all versions up through the TBM-3. On a few -1D and -3D aircraft, these were moved to the top of each wing. TBM-3Es used the APS-4 radar instead. *(National Archives)*

The flaps on the trailing edge of the right wing can be seen here. On Avengers painted in the tri-color scheme, the inside of the flap well was painted white, but the inside of the flap was Sea Blue.

Each flap was divided at the wing fold into inner and outer sections. This is the outer flap on the left wing.

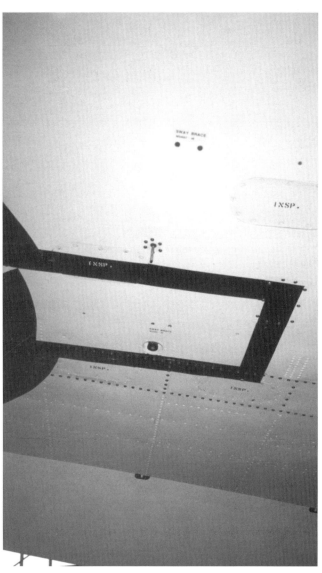

The temperature probe can be seen just forward of the national insignia. This view looks aft under the right wing.

The inner flap on the left wing is shown here as is the natural metal link that joined the inner and outer sections together.

The wings on the Avenger folded in much the same manner as on the Hellcat and later versions of the Wildcat. At left, the wings are shown during the folding process, while at right is a rear view which reveals just how compact the aircraft became when the wings were completely folded. Vought's F4U Corsair and the Curtiss SB2C Helldiver both had wings that folded up over the aircraft. But Grumman's concept of folding the wings horizontally along the aircraft's sides minimized the vertical dimension, and this was important on the hangar decks aboard ship. This feature helped make the relatively large Avenger suitable for operations aboard even the smallest escort carriers. (Both National Archives)

Details of the right wing fold mechanism can be seen here.

This view looks over the leading edge of the left wing and shows the aft cross section of the outer wing panel.

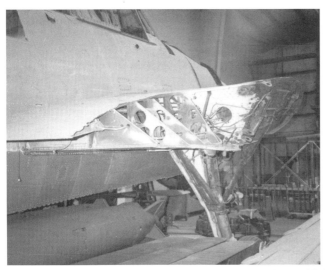

One of only two remaining Grumman-built TBF-1s is awaiting restoration at the Yanks Air Museum at Chino, California. With the wings removed, it is easy to study the design of the right wing fold assembly and hinge.

Just aft of the navigation light on each wing was a small compartment that housed a short cable. The cable was attached to a small anchor point on the leading edge of the horizontal stabilizer to help hold the wing in the folded position. At left is the top of the compartment on the right wing tip. Note the stencilling on the top door. The photograph at right shows the compartment with both doors open. The interior of the compartment was painted Interior Green.

This inside view shows the cable extending from the right wing tip to the leading edge of the horizontal stabilizer.

The anchor point where the tie-back cable was attached to the leading edge of the right horizontal stabilizer can be seen just inboard of the elevator.

TAIL DETAILS

Details of the vertical stabilizer and rudder are shown in these two photographs. Note that the two-section trim tab on the rudder is controlled by actuators on the right side. There is a white position light on the trailing edge of the fabric-covered rudder. A small mast at the top of the rudder is the aft connecting point for the wire antenna.

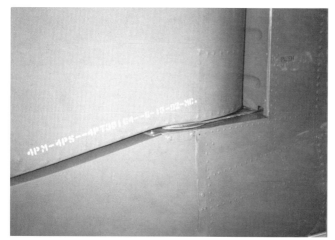

The control cable for the rudder was located at its base. It exited the vertical stabilizer, extended around a grooved wheel at the base of the rudder, and re-entered the vertical stabilizer on the opposite side.

A builder's plate was attached to the tail section just under the left horizontal stabilizer. Note the electrical connection running between the aft fuselage and the rudder.

A trim tab was located on each elevator. The one on the left elevator was controlled by an actuator on top, while the one on the right elevator had its actuator on the underside.

Most Avengers had the internal arresting hook as shown here. When retracted, only a couple of inches of the aft end were exposed.

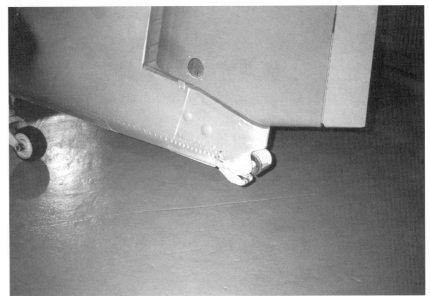

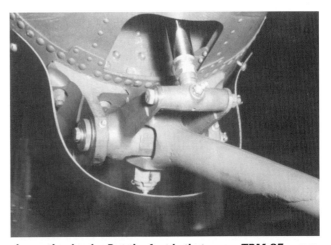

It has been reported elsewhere that the TBM-3E had an external arresting hook. But the fact is that many TBM-3Es were built with the internal hook illustrated above. The change to the external hook did not occur until the production of BuNo. 86175 which was well into the production of the -3E variant. At left is the external hook in the retracted position, while at right is a close-up of the attachment point. This fixed attachment point was sturdier and less prone to failure than the sliding internal hook. It was also easier to maintain, and there were less corrosion problems.

(Both Eastern)

MODELERS SECTION

1/144th SCALE KIT

Academy/Minicraft TBF Avenger

Originally released by Crown, this model is now marketed under the Academy/Minicraft label. It has been released in medium blue and silver plastic, and it consists of twenty-three pieces. Five of these are clear parts that include a canopy, turret, stinger gun window, and windows for the sides of the fuselage.

As is the case with several Avenger models, this kit is a hybrid of variants. The cowling has only the top scoop which indicates a -1 or -1C. But the cowl flaps are those found on a TBM-3. Neither the single .30-caliber cowl gun of the TBF-1 nor the .50-caliber wing guns of later versions are represented. Also missing is the stinger gun. But any of these weapons could easily be added from scratch in this small scale. The markings are for an early TBF-1 with the codes 8-T-3 on the fuselage sides. Included are the red and white stripes for the rudder. An aircraft with these markings would have been an early -1 which had the small round window in the aft crew entry door. However, this feature is not represented in the kit.

There is no cockpit detailing, and some basic features could easily be added from plastic card. Likewise, there is no representation of the engine details inside the cowling. Both extended and retracted landing gear is provided, but there is no stand on which to mount the model if the gear is built in the retracted position.

Assembly is simple and illustrated in three drawings on one side of the instruction sheet. On the reverse is information about the markings and paint scheme. In the two sample kits we reviewed, one had information for the markings of a P-47 Thunderbolt, while the other correctly showed the Avenger. The fit is generally good, with only a small amount of filler being needed where the wings and horizontal tails join the fuselage.

The basic shape, outline, and size of the Avenger is represented very well by this kit. With the easy addition of some missing details, this model can be built into a very nice replica. The modeler will have to add or change some

The only Avenger available in 1/144th scale is the former Crown kit which is now marketed under the Academy/ Minicraft label. For the most part, the model represents a TBM-3, but the markings provided are for one of the TBF-1s that participated in the Battle of Midway. **(Gold)**

features to build a specific variant, but considering the cowl flaps, a TBF-3 would be the easiest to build.

Paul Gold contributed to this review.

1/100th SCALE KIT

Aoshima TBF-1

The box art claims that this kit is 1/72nd scale, but it is noticeably too small. A quick measurement of the parts indicates that it is closer to 1/100th scale instead.

The kit is molded in light gray plastic except for the two clear parts that represent the canopy and turret. Side windows and the windows for the stinger gun position are simply indentions in the plastic. Surface detailing is represented by raised rivets and panel lines, and there are numerous inaccuracies. Most obvious is that the crew entry door is scribed on both sides of the fuselage. The "mail box" slots on the wings are slanted backwards from the direction they should be.

The details that are present are very crude, and this includes toy-like wings that fold. The engine and landing gear are likewise very poorly represented. The main wheel wells are far too shallow to accommodate the gear. There are considerable shape problems as well, and these prevent this kit from being used to build an accurate scale model.

1/72nd SCALE KITS

Academy/Minicraft TBF Avenger

This model has a lot in common with the old Frog Tarpon II kit covered below. In fact, it would be fair to say that it is a descendant of the Frog model. While some noteworthy improvements have been made, several features remain the same as in the Frog kit, and these include some of the mistakes.

This Academy/Minicraft kit is a cross between a TBF-1 and a TBF-1C, or more correctly, a Tarpon I and a Tarpon II. However, it has neither the .30-caliber cowl gun found on the TBF-1 nor the .50-caliber wing guns fitted to all subsequent variants. It has the second cockpit as used in the TBF-1 and British Tarpons, but it was not in any American Avengers after the TBF-1. The antenna mast is placed on the canopy in the position where it would be for the TBF-1C and subsequent versions. A feature that limits the kit's value is that the only clear parts for the forward fuselage windows are the larger blistered scanning windows used on the British aircraft. Surprisingly, the instructions show these blisters being fitted to the inside of the fuselage halves. They should go on the outside. To build a U. S. version, the modeler will have to make new standard windows from clear plastic to fit in the oversized holes. Epoxy these windows in place, sand them smooth, then polish them. Once this is done, mask the window off in the correct size and shape, then paint the fuselage.

To build a TBF-1, add the cowl gun, move the antenna mast forward and angle it slightly rearward, and replace the blistered windows with flat ones. To build a TBF-1C, remove the seat and consoles from the rear

The Academy/Minicraft Avenger in 1/72nd scale is a hybrid with the features of several different variants mixed together. This includes the blistered side windows as used on the British aircraft. This model was built as a Fleet Air Arm Tarpon II by Jim Roeder. (Roeder)

cockpit and replace them with some radio gear made from plastic card. Add the blisters to the top of the wings for the wing guns, then drill holes in the leading edge of each wing where the gun blast tubes would be. Finally, replace the blistered side windows with flat ones for all U. S. aircraft.

Detailing leaves a lot to be desired. The wheel wells are devoid of any interiors, and the cockpits are not much better. There is a seat for each cockpit, and a control column is provided for the pilot's cockpit. Side consoles are molded on the floors, but not even decals are included to represent the details. A loop antenna is provided, but it was not used in Avengers.

Detailing inside the turret is likewise sparse and inaccurate. There is no representation of the tail hook, and the YAGI antennas have only the strut and center piece. The probes are missing. These would be very fragile in this scale, so we recommend using one of the available 1/72nd scale brass detailing sets that include these antennas instead. The engine details are molded inside the cowl ring, and this also leaves something to be desired.

The landing gear can be built in the extended or retracted position, and a stand is provided if the model is built in a gear-up configuration. The weapons bay doors are molded in the closed position, so there is no option for showing the bay open with weapons loaded.

The canopy is one piece, and it has the clear divider just forward of the turret. The framework is a little too thick, and there should be no vertical frame on the pilot's right sliding panel. Likewise, the framework on the turret is both inaccurate and incomplete. The aft-most triangular window on each side of the stinger gun position is incorrect and needs to be reworked. Refer to the photographs in this book to make the necessary corrections.

Shapes are generally good, except that the leading edge of the vertical tail is noticeably too rounded. Considering the inaccuracies and lack of detailing in this kit, we recommend using the better Hasegawa models when building a 1/72nd scale Avenger or Tarpon.

Jim Roeder contributed to this review.

Airfix/MPC TBM-3

This kit has been issued many times under both the Airfix and MPC labels, and it is now over thirty years old. It is covered with rivets and raised panel lines that detract from the model. These will have to be sanded off, and new panel lines will have to be scribed in.

Fit is poor, and a lot of filling and sanding will be required during construction. A number of sink marks and ejector pin marks will likewise have to be filled and sanded as well. The ailerons are separate parts, as they were on many Airfix kits from the 1960s, and this causes fit problems as well. Some modelers may want to fill in the cracks and rescribe these parts.

The features of the kit faithfully represent the TBM-3 configuration except that the cowl flaps are more like those found on the TBM-3E. The second cockpit has a representation of radio gear in it rather than a second seat, and the stinger gun position is likewise included. Very crude figures are provided for the pilot, turret gunner, and the radio operator who is posed manning the tunnel gun. The YAGI antennas look more like pitot probes, because the cross probes are missing. As with the Academy/Minicraft kit, these would be very tiny in this scale, and they could be built from scratch using sprue. Aftermarket brass parts are also available.

Detailing is practically non-existent. There are no interiors for the wheel wells, and only a seat and control column are provided for the pilot's cockpit. Nothing more than a very simple machine gun and base are included for the turret. The weapons bay doors are molded in the closed position, so there is no bay interior or weapons. Eight rockets are included to go under the wings, however their fins are molded in the incorrect + configuration rather than as an X as they should be.

The engine does come as two rows of cylinders, and while this is better than having it molded into the cowling, the execution of the cylinders is not very good.

The canopy is all one piece, and it is fairly thick. However, the framework that has been scribed on it is thin and more in scale than that found on the Academy/Minicraft kit. But it also has the vertical framework on the pilot's right sliding panel which does not belong there. Other clear parts are provided for the side windows, retractable landing light, and the windows for the tunnel gun position.

Shapes and dimensions are generally good, and the

The old Airfix kit represents a TBM-3, but it has the external tail hook. This model was built by Stan Parker and was painted in the Dark Gull Gray over white scheme used in the Atlantic. (Parker)

finished model does not have any noticeable problems as far as accuracy is concerned. The best word to describe this kit is "basic," and it is very typical of kits from the late 1950s and early -60s. Again, we recommend using the better Hasegawa models which are covered below.

Stan Parker contributed to this review.

Frog Avenger Mk II

Now forty years old, the Frog Avenger Mk II kit is probably the oldest of all 1/72nd scale Avengers. It shows its age with its lack of detail and crude molding. There are a number of inaccuracies with respect to shape and outline. With much better 1/72nd scale Avenger kits available from Hasegawa, these old Frog models only have value to collectors.

Hasegawa TBF/TBM-1C & Tarpon Mk II

These kits have already been released several times, and more issues are sure to follow if Hasegawa remains true to its form of reissuing the same kit numerous times. But these Hasegawa models, along with their TBM-3 counterparts, are the best of the Avenger kits in 1/72nd scale. They are the most accurate, best detailed, and they offer the most options of any Avenger kits in this scale.

The kits are molded in light gray plastic, and the panel lines are fine, accurate, and recessed. Fit is excellent, and only a very small amount of filling and sanding is required.

Optional weapons bay doors allow the model to be built with the doors opened or closed. The closed set of doors fit perfectly and will require no filling or sanding. For modelers who choose the open position, Hasegawa has provided a basic interior with an early style torpedo to go inside. Unfortunately, there are no options for later generation torpedoes or any bombs, but these can be obtained from other kits.

There is a considerable gap running down the entire length of the top of the weapons bay. Although the torpedo will cover some of this gap, it is best to properly close and fill it during construction. The small window between the radio compartment and the aft end of the bomb bay is missing, and this was on most Avengers. It would be easy to open up the appropriate hole and fill it with a piece of clear plastic or some Kristal Kleer.

Up front, the engine is the best in any 1/72nd scale Avenger model, but it still falls short of expectations for today's models. Both rows of cylinders are molded as one piece, and the aft row is too close to the front row. Aftermarket engines are available and will look much better than what comes in the kit.

Another problem exists with the cockpit interior. Hasegawa provided a seat for the second cockpit, and only the TBF-1 and British Tarpons had this seat. So for the -1C, the seat must be removed and replaced with scratchbuilt radio gear. The crawlway between this area and the radio compartment must be opened up on the right side. The pilot's cockpit is basic, with an instrument panel, control column, and seat being included. Side consoles are molded as part of the floor. Decals are provided for the instrument panel and consoles. Aftermarket sets are available from Hi Tech, Aires, and Kendall,

The best Avenger kits in 1/72nd scale are from Hasegawa. Various releases have been issued that represent the TBF-1C and TBM-3 versions. Jim Roeder completed this model as a TBF-1C and painted it in the two-tone Atlantic scheme. *(Roeder)*

and all of these have the correct floor and middle cockpit with the radios.

The interior of the turret is not completely accurate, but a nice feature is that the turret can be installed after the model is otherwise finished and painted.

Again, and because of the small scale, the YAGI antennas are missing the cross pieces. We would recommend replacing these with brass parts from an aftermarket set.

The clear parts are thin, but Hasegawa made the same mistake as several other companies by scribing a vertical frame on the pilot's right sliding panel. Clear parts are also included for the fuselage side windows, the retractable landing light under the left wing, and the stinger gun position. All issues of the kit come with two clear parts for the stinger gun position, and according to the instructions, one is for the TBF-1C, and the other is for the TBM-3 versions. However, the piece for the -3 should be used regardless. Adding a small piece of clear plastic on each side of the lip will produce the correct appearance for the TBF-1C.

These kits come with rockets, but they are mounted on stubs. This is the arrangement used on TBM-3s and TBM-3Es, so be sure not to use them on a TBF-1C. This version carried rockets on launch rails instead.

Although not entirely accurate, interiors are molded into the main gear wells, and they add significantly to the appearance of the finished model when compared to the Airfix/MPC and Academy/Minicraft kits.

The issue which represents a Royal Navy Tarpon Mk II is identical to the TBF-1C issue except for the decals provided. Use the seat in the second cockpit and the blistered fuselage windows when building a Tarpon.

Hasegawa TBM-3

The Hasegawa TBM-3 kits are basically the same as the TBF-1Cs covered above. A different cowl lip with the lower scoop has been added, and this is correct for the -3 variants. The cowl flap arrangement has been changed to include the flaps that extended all the way down to the exhausts on each side. But Hasegawa provided the flaps as used on the TBM-3E version instead of the -3. The cowl flaps are all of equal width, but for the TBM-3, the ones at the bottom should be slightly indented. See the drawings and photographs in this book for the correct configuration of the cowl flaps for both versions. It will be fairly easy to modify the flaps as necessary when building a TBM-3.

As with its TBF-1C kits, Hasegawa also included the seat for the second cockpit. This does not belong in the TBM-3 or TBM-3E versions. Hasegawa also did not provide the different instrument panel with the flat top as used in the later variants. A little work will be necessary to correct the kit part to the proper shape.

It would be a simple matter to build a TBM-3E from one of the TBM-3 releases by Hasegawa. The lower cowl flaps are already correct for the TBM-3E as mentioned before. The hole in the ventral window for the stinger gun would have to be filled in, and the framework should be sanded off. The part should then be painted the same color as the surrounding fuselage. An external tail hook can be added from the parts box if required for the specific TBM-3E being modeled, and the pod for the APS-4 radar can be obtained from Hasegawa's F6F-3E kit.

For any modeler wishing to build a 1/72nd scale model of an Avenger, these Hasegawa kits are the place to start. Although they have some shortcomings, they are superior to the other 1/72nd scale Avengers.

Stan Parker and Jim Roeder contributed to this review.

1/48th SCALE KITS

Accurate Miniatures Avengers

There is an old adage that states, "Good things comes to those who wait." In the scale aircraft modeling community, these Avengers from Accurate Miniatures are prime examples that this saying is true. This relatively new U. S. model company received a lot of criticism when these and other kits were delayed a considerable amount of time past their originally announced released dates. But in late 1996, the four Avenger kits finally appeared on the shelves of hobby shops, and the excellent quality of the kits was certainly worth the wait. Not only are these the best Avenger models in any scale, they are among the finest plastic model airplane kits ever released.

We will review the first release, kit number 3403, in detail and then follow this review with separate explanations of what is different in the other three kits.

Accurate Miniatures TBF-1C, Kit Number 3403

Much research went into the development of this model, and it shows in the exquisite detailing throughout. In the cockpit, engine, wheel wells, and weapons bay, the quality and amount of detailing is equivalent to what is usually found in expensive after-market sets. By providing this level of detail in a reasonably priced kit, Accurate Miniatures has pushed forward the quality of work that the average modeler can accomplish from a kit right out of the box. For this they should be complimented.

At the front of the aircraft is a superb engine with two rows of cylinders and a crankcase. Molded with the crankcase is a nicely detailed ignition wiring harness. It is probably the best radial engine ever included in a 1/48th

scale model.

Moving further aft, the cockpit has more extensive detailing than found on some after-market sets. The only noticeable item that is missing is the pilot's relief tube. As with previous kits from Accurate Miniatures, the instrument panel is molded in clear plastic, and there are optional ways it can be painted so that the instruments appear to be covered by glass faces.

One point should be made here about the instrument panel. The clear tree of parts has two instrument panels in all four kits. On both kits of the TBF-1C (3403 and 3405) the instructions are very confusing concerning which panel to use. Both indicate part number 65 which is the instrument panel with the curved top. But in the drawings, the instrument panel with the flat top (part 66) is represented. For TBF-1Cs, the panel with the curved top (part 65) is the correct one to use, and for the TBF-3 version, the panel with the flat top (part 66) is correct.

The turret and radio operator's station is likewise well detailed. Even the flare tubes in the aft cockpit are provided. Throughout the interior, care should be taken during assembly and painting in order to obtain the best results from the excellent detailing that Accurate Miniatures has provided. The crew entry door can be assembled in the open position to reveal the interior of the radio compartment.

The weapons bay is the best we have seen on any plastic model. The features of its interior, including the bi-fold doors, are exquisitely represented from end to end. The actuating mechanisms for the doors are included, and they are both delicate and accurate replicas of the real thing. Even the small window between the aft fuselage compartment and the bomb bay is included as a clear part.

In this kit, which has markings for an aircraft from the escort carrier USS BLOCK ISLAND, CVE-21, two depth bombs and two general purpose bombs are included to go inside the weapons bay. This would be a typical load for the Avengers that flew from the decks of the escort carriers to hunt U-boats in the Atlantic.

The canopy is thin and very clear. All scribing is accurate and in scale. The two sliding panels that cover the pilot's cockpit are separate pieces, and the right panel correctly does not have the vertical frame in the center. Other clear parts include the aft fuselage windows, and even the blistered windows used on the British aircraft are provided. The turret halves, wing tip lights, retractable landing light, gun sight, and the windows for the tunnel gun are also on the tree of clear parts, and each is very well executed.

Two sets of main landing gear tires are included. One has the parallel groves in the tire, and the second set has the diamond tread pattern. As with the rest of the kit, the landing gear is exceptionally well reproduced, and the wheel wells have accurate interiors.

The exterior of the model is as well done as the interior. The surface detailing is both accurate and complete, except that the three identification lights under the fuselage are missing. Every other feature has been scribed in magnificent detail that is realistic in every respect.

There is only one serious shortcoming of this kit, and that is the instruction sheet. The line drawings are poor, and in several cases, it is not clear how the parts actually go together. We strongly recommend test fitting all parts to make absolutely sure how they join before applying any cement. Be particularly careful with how part 25 mates to part 19. Make sure you understand where the bomb racks (parts 84L, 84R, 85L, 85R, 86L and 86R) fit inside the bomb bay. Other parts that require extra study before assembly are 33, 36, 37, 52, and 53. Also, be sure not to put the front row of cylinders (part 8) in backwards. The alignment pins are the same for the crankcase as they are for the rear row of cylinders. A good recommendation is to study the detailed photographs in this book for each area being assembled to help understand how the parts go together.

With the exception of the instructions, it would be difficult to find a better scale model kit on the market today. The only ones we would rate as being superior would be the Accurate Miniatures Dauntlesses, but that would be by a very narrow margin. The perfect kit has never been produced and probably never will be. But these models from Accurate Miniatures push the standard of excellence another step forward over anything that has come before.

Accurate Miniatures TBF-1C, Kit Number 3405

This kit is essentially the same as kit number 3403 covered immediately above. The differences are the weapons included to go inside the bomb bay and the decals. Markings are for a TBF-1C from VT-10 which operated from the USS ENTERPRISE, CV-6. On February 10, 1944, this aircraft was one of several Avengers that participated in a raid on the Japanese anchorage at Truk Lagoon. Accurate Miniatures likes to include markings in its kits that capture a specific moment in history, and they have done this with their Avenger models.

The Avengers that participated in the raid on Truk Lagoon that day carried four 500-pound bombs, and these are the weapons provided in this particular kit.

It is also noteworthy that Accurate Miniatures is the only company so far to point out the use of Bronze Green in the cockpit interiors of Grumman-built Avengers. This is one example of the considerable research this manufacturer puts into its kits.

The second TBF-1C released by Accurate Miniatures came with markings for an Avenger from VT-10 aboard the USS ENTERPRISE. Armament in this kit includes four 500-pound general purpose bombs. The kit number is 3405.

Accurate Miniatures TBM-3, Kit Number 3404

All of the differences between the TBF-1C and the TBM-3 have been faithfully represented in this kit when compared to the two TBF-1Cs covered above. The additional scoop at the bottom of the cowling, the different cowl flap arrangement, and the different instrument panel are all provided. Armament in this kit consists of four 500-pound general purpose bombs or a 1600-pound armor-piercing bomb to go in the weapons bay. Eight 5-inch rockets are also included to go under the wings.

Markings are provided for a TBM-3 from VT-84 which is painted in the tri-color scheme. This Avenger operated from the USS BUNKER HILL, CV-17, during attacks against Okinawa in early April 1945.

Accurate Miniatures TBM-3, Kit Number 3406

Most of the features in this kit are the same as those in kit number 3404 above. The bombs and rockets have been replaced by a torpedo, and three versions of the Mk 13 can be built using optional parts. Primary markings are for an overall Sea Blue Avenger which was assigned to VT-10. In April 1945, this squadron was operating from the USS INTREPID, CV-11, and this particular TBM-3 took part in the attack which sunk the IJN light cruiser YAHAGI on April 7.

Optional parts are included for the wing-mounted radome as used on TBM-3Ds. If these parts are used, a second set of markings is provided for a night bomber from VT(N)-90. This unit operated from the USS ENTERPRISE, CV-6, in early 1945. These same parts could also be used with one of the Accurate Miniatures TBF-1C kits to build a TBF-1D.

Lindberg TBM-3 Avenger

Initially released in the 1950s, this model is still being marketed by Lindberg. The most recent issue has markings for George Bush's *Barbara III*, but that aircraft was a TBM-1C, and the kit represents a TBM-3.

As was the case with most larger plastic models from the 1950s, this kit came with a lot of working features. The first issue had the option of rigging the control stick to the rudder and elevators so they would work. Other operating features included a retractable landing gear, moveable canopies, bomb bay doors that opened and closed, and a moveable rear access door. Of course, the propeller spinned and the wheels rolled.

Weapons consisted of an ASW Fido torpedo, two depth bombs, and eight rockets. One issue also included the radar pod so that a TBM-3D variant could be built.

Although the Monogram kit (reviewed next) has always been more popular, this offering from Lindberg provides better detailing. The interior is reasonably complete in the cockpit and the gun turret, and a basic interior of the bomb bay is also provided. While this detailing is not really accurate, it is much better and more complete than that found in the Monogram kit, and it offers a better starting point for anyone wanting to do some detailing work. The engine has two separate rows of cylinders, and this is better than the single-piece unit of the Monogram model. While Monogram had a one-piece canopy, this Lindberg model came with a canopy that could be displayed in the open or closed position.

Stan Parker modified the old 1/48th scale Lindberg kit to build this TBM-3E. The markings are for an Avenger from VMTB-132 which operated from the USS CAPE GLOUCESTER, CVE-109, during July 1945. (Parker)

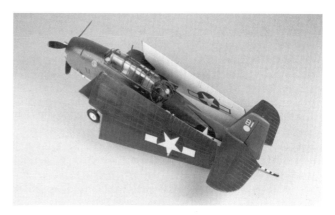

Even with the release of the Accurate Miniatures kits, the old Monogram Avenger remains the only TBF-1 in 1/48th scale. It is crude by today's standards and has many toy-like features. Stan Parker modified this Monogram kit to represent a TBF-1C from VT-12 and the USS HORNET, CV-12. (Parker)

On the negative side, the propeller hub is too blunt and the blades are too pointed. The radio operator's station is not detailed at all, with only the rough outline of a seat being provided to glue onto the side of the fuselage. This reduces the value of having a moveable rear access door, because there is nothing to display if the door is left open. The pitot probe is not accurate in shape or location. The wheels are thin and are best replaced with ones from True Details. The weapons leave something to be desired and should be replaced with ones from other kits. This includes the under-wing rockets as well as the weapons for the bomb bay.

Surprisingly, the kit goes together quite well, and only a modest amount of filling and sanding is required. Compared to other kits from the 1950s it is reasonably accurate in shape and outline, and it has a better than average interior detail. But by today's standards, this model falls well short of what is expected as far as accuracy and detailing are concerned.

Stan Parker contributed to this review.

Monogram TBF-1 Avenger

Initially released more than forty years ago, Monogram's Avenger remains today as the only kit available of a TBF-1 in 1/48th scale. In fact, it is the only model in any scale that has a representation of the .30-caliber machine gun on the cowling.

On the outside, its shape and outline are basically correct, and its raised surface detailing is fine and crisp. But on the inside, it is much more of a toy than a scale model. Working features include a retractable landing gear, folding wings, bomb bay doors that open, a droppable torpedo, wheels that roll, a propeller than spins, and a turret that rotates with a machine gun that moves up and down.

While the overall outline of this kit may be better than Lindberg's model, it falls short of the Lindberg offering when it comes to detailing. There is no cockpit interior, no detailing in the turret or radio compartment, and no features represented in the wheel wells or wing fold areas.

The bomb bay doors do not open as the real ones do, being only one-piece on each side instead of the correct bi-fold doors. The engine is molded inside the cowling, but the forward row of cylinders looks fairly good.

As far as the shape and outline are concerned, this was the most accurate 1/48th scale Avenger model available until the Accurate Miniatures kits were released in late 1996. Because of this, Medalion Models released a detailing set of resin, metal, and etched brass which was designed specifically for this kit. It consisted of eighty parts, considerably more than the model itself, and it could be used to super detail and correct the Monogram kit. Among the parts included were a new cowl lip, complete engine, cockpit interior, bomb bay interior and doors, turret detailing, complete landing gear, and interiors for the wheel wells. Detailing where the wings fold was also included, so the model could be built with wings folded and still look very realistic. Using the Medalion detailing set, an experienced modeler could turn this kit into a very nice replica of a TBF-1. Although this detailing set is no longer available, we would recommend finding one at a swap meet and using it if any modeler wanted to build a TBF-1 from this kit. Without this detailing set, trying to build a quality model from this kit would take a lot of scratchbuilding and many hours of work.

The canopy is molded as one piece, and the sliding panel on the pilot's right side correctly does not have the vertical framing that is found in several other kits. But the same vertical framework is also missing from the left side, and it should be there. The mounting for the antenna mast on top of the canopy is in the position where it would be on TBF-1Cs and all subsequent Avengers. This is the one place where the model departs from the characteristics of the TBF-1.

For modelers who remember this Monogram kit from their childhood, it has a nostalgic value. But realistically, this is the only value it has. When it comes to building a model today, converting an Accurate Miniatures TBF-1C to a TBF-1 would be far easier than attempting to build this kit even with the Medalion Models detailing set.

Stan Parker contributed to this review.